For Engineers & Designers

OpenSCAD Exercises

200 3D PRACTICE DRAWINGS

SACHIDANAND JHA

Dear Reader,

Thank you for choosing **OpenSCAD Exercises** book. This book is part of a family of premium-quality CADIN360 books, all of which are written by Outstanding author who combine practical experience with a gift for teaching.

CADIN360 was founded in 2016. More than 3 years later, we're still committed to producing consistently exceptional books. With each of our titles, we're working hard to set a new standard for the industry. From the paper we print on, to the authors we work with, our goal is to bring you the best books available.

I hope you see all that reflected in these pages. I'd be very interested to hear your comments and get your feedback on how we're doing. Feel free to let me know what you think about this or any other CADIN360 book by sending me an email at contactus@cadin360.com.

If you think you've found a technical error in this book, please visit https://cadin360.com/contact-us/.
Customer feedback is critical to our efforts at CADIN360.

Best regards,

Sachidanand Jha
Founder & CEO, CADIN360

OpenSCAD Exercises

Published by
CADIN360
cadin360.com

Limit of Liability/Disclaimer of Warranty:

Examination Copies

Electronic Files

Disclaimer:

Preface

OpenSCAD Exercises

❖ This book contain 200 CAD practice exercises and drawings.

❖ This book does not provide step by step tutorial to design 3D models.

❖ S.I Unit is used.

❖ Predominantly used Third Angle Projection.

❖ This book is for **OpenSCAD** and Other Feature-Based Modeling Software such as Inventor, SolidWorks, NX, Solid Edge, AutoCAD, PTC Creo etc.

❖ It is intended to provide Drafters, Designers and Engineers with enough 3D CAD exercises for practice on **OpenSCAD**.

❖ It includes almost all types of exercises that are necessary to provide, clear, concise and systematic information required on industrial machine part drawings.

❖ Third Angle Projection is intentionally used to familiarize Drafters, Designers and Engineers in Third Angle Projection to meet the expectation of world wide Engineering drawing print.

❖ Clear and well drafted drawing help easy understanding of the design.

❖ This book is for Beginner, Intermediate and Advance CAD users.

❖ These exercises are from Basics to Advance level.

❖ Each exercises can be assigned and designed separately.

❖ No Exercise is a prerequisite for another. All dimensions are in mm.

❖ Note: Assume any missing dimensions.

EX-01

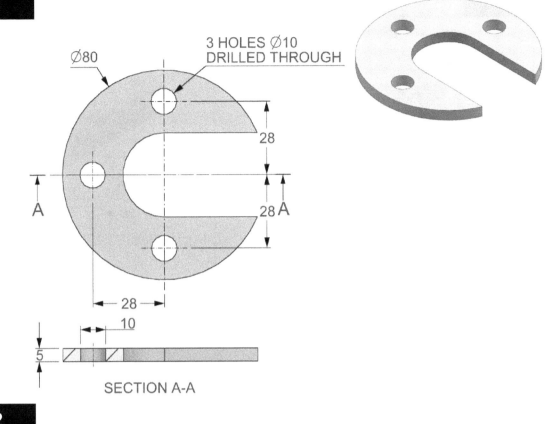

Ø80

3 HOLES Ø10
DRILLED THROUGH

28

28

A · · A

28

10

5

SECTION A-A

EX-02

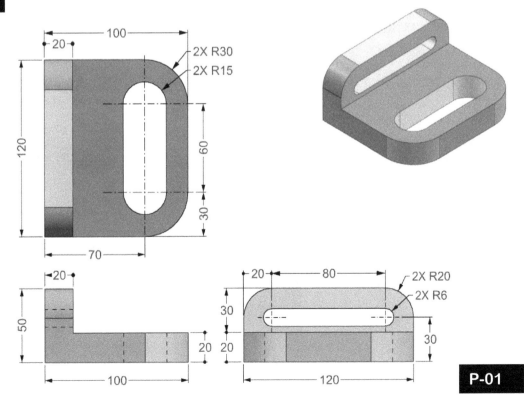

100

20

2X R30

2X R15

120

60

30

70

20

50

100

20

20

2X R20

2X R6

30

30

20

120

80

P-01

EX-03

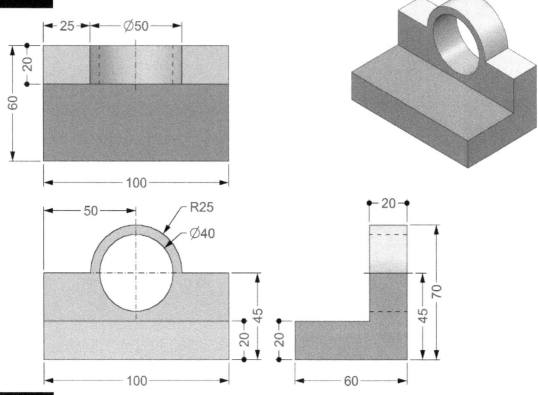

- 25
- Ø50
- 20
- 60
- 100

- 50
- R25
- Ø40
- 45
- 20
- 100

- 20
- 70
- 45
- 20
- 60

EX-04`

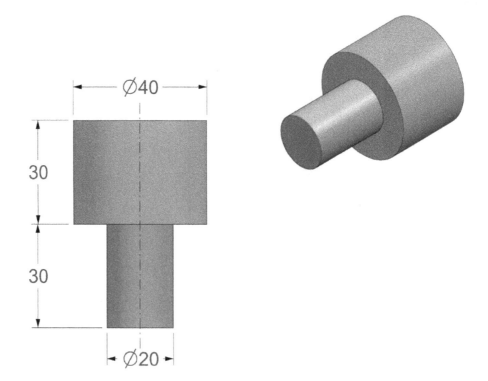

- Ø40
- 30
- 30
- Ø20

P-02

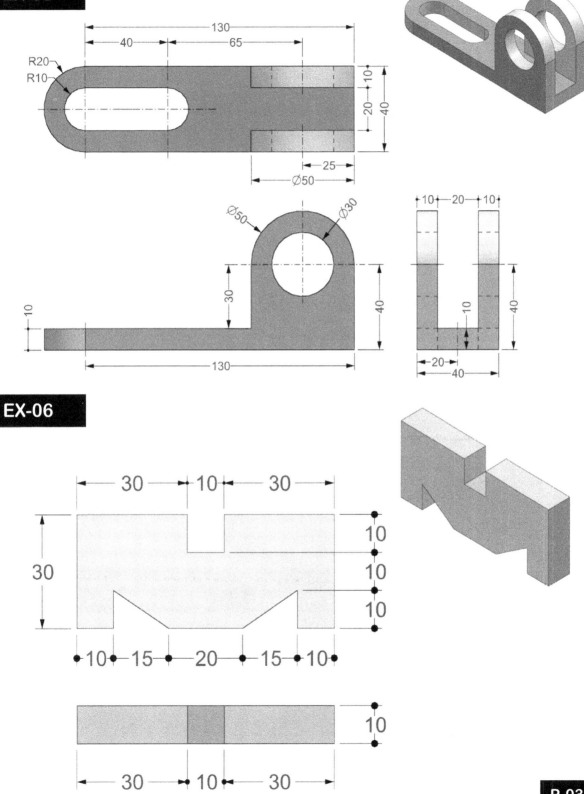

EX-05

R20
R10

130
40
65
40
20
10
25
Ø50

Ø50
Ø30
30
40
10
130

10 20 10
40
10
20
40

EX-06

30 10 30
30
10
10
10
10 15 20 15 10

10
30 10 30

P-03

EX-07

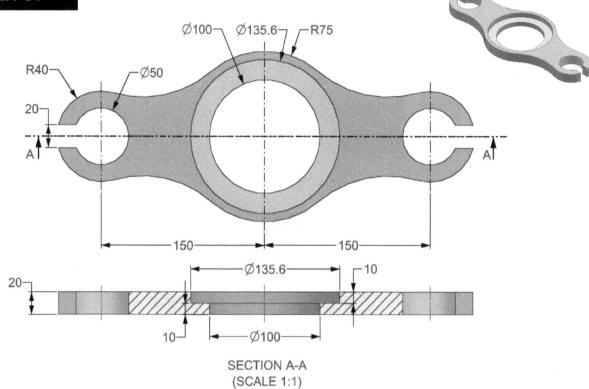

Ø100 Ø135.6 R75

R40 Ø50

20

A

A

150 150

Ø135.6 10

20

10 Ø100

SECTION A-A
(SCALE 1:1)

EX-08

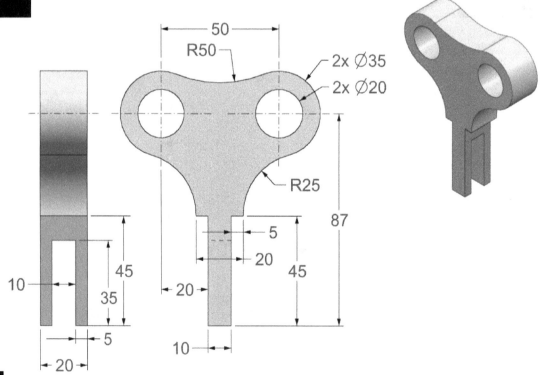

50

R50

2x Ø35

2x Ø20

R25

87

5

20

45

45

20

10

10

45

35

5

20

P-04

EX-09

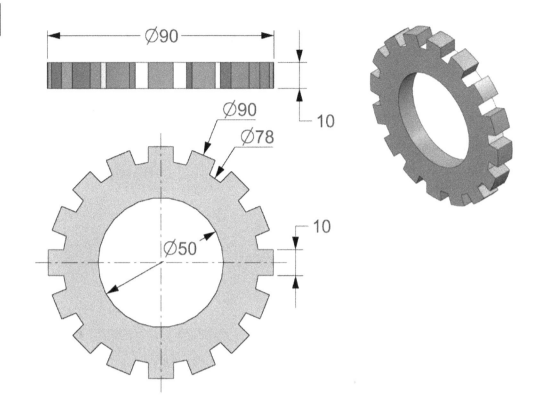

Ø90

Ø90
Ø78

10

Ø50

10

EX-10

50
40

R15
Ø12
Ø30

Ø15

Ø20

A

40

40

R50

A

85

Ø40
R30

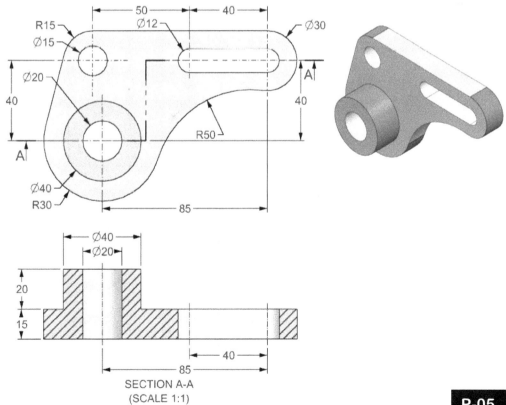

Ø40
Ø20

20

15

40

85

SECTION A-A
(SCALE 1:1)

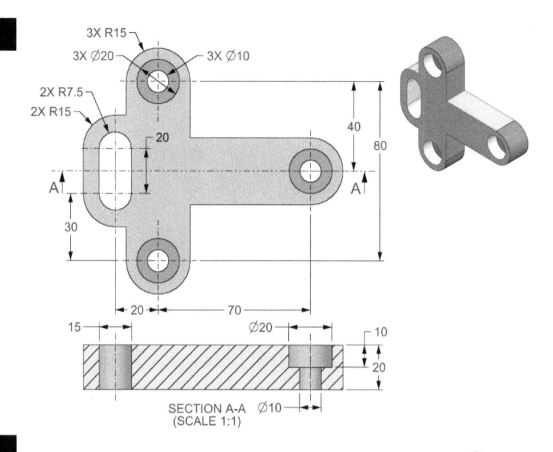

3X R15
3X Ø20
3X Ø10
2X R7.5
2X R15
20
40
80
A
A
30
20
70

15
Ø20
10
20
SECTION A-A
(SCALE 1:1)
Ø10

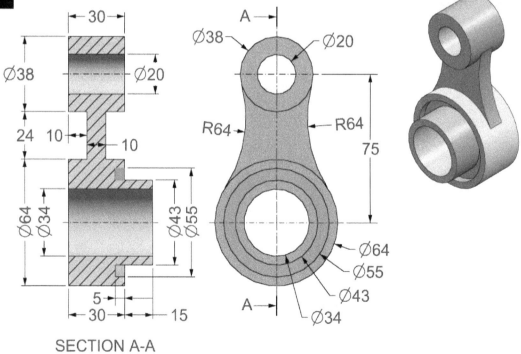

30
Ø38
Ø20
24 10
10
Ø64 Ø34
Ø43 Ø55
5
30
15

A
Ø38
Ø20
R64
R64
75
Ø64
Ø55
Ø43
Ø34
A

SECTION A-A
(SCALE 1:1)

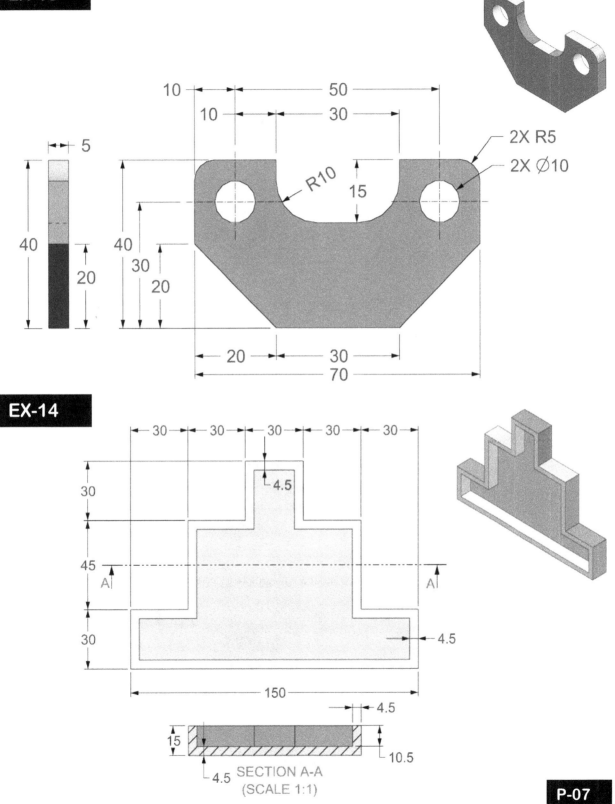

EX-13

5

10 | 50
10 | 30

2X R5
2X Ø10

R10
15

40
40
30
20
20

20 | 30
70

EX-14

30 | 30 | 30 | 30 | 30

30
4.5

45
A | A

30

150

4.5
15 | 10.5
4.5
SECTION A-A
(SCALE 1:1)

P-07

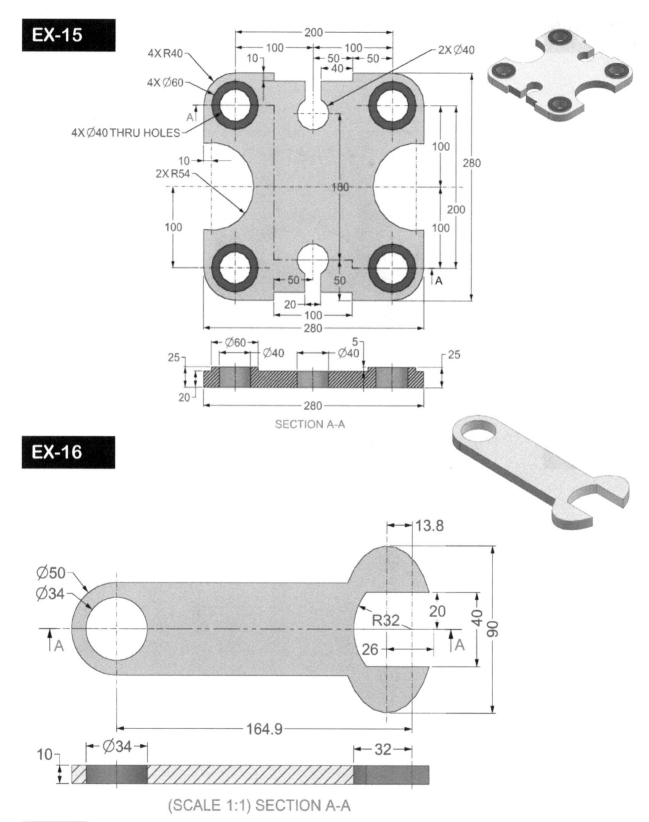

EX-15

4X R40
4X Ø60
4X Ø40 THRU HOLES
2X R54
2X Ø40

200
100
100
10
50
50
40
10
100
280
180
200
100
100
50
50
20
100
280

SECTION A-A

Ø60
Ø40
Ø40
5
25
25
25
20
280

EX-16

Ø50
Ø34

13.8
R32
20
40
26
90

164.9

Ø34
32
10

(SCALE 1:1) SECTION A-A

P-08

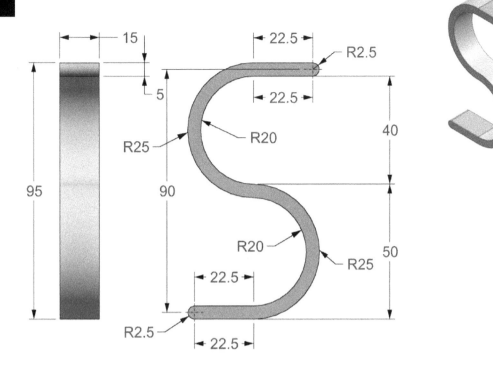

15
22.5
R2.5
22.5
5
R25
R20
40
95
90
R20
50
R25
22.5
R2.5
22.5

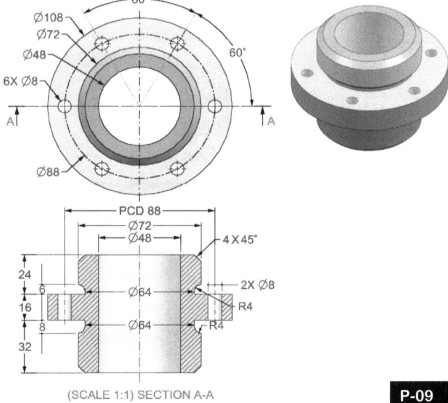

60°
Ø108
Ø72
Ø48
60°
6X Ø8
Ø88

PCD 88
Ø72
Ø48
4 X 45°
24
6
Ø64
2X Ø8
16
R4
8
Ø64
R4
32

(SCALE 1:1) SECTION A-A

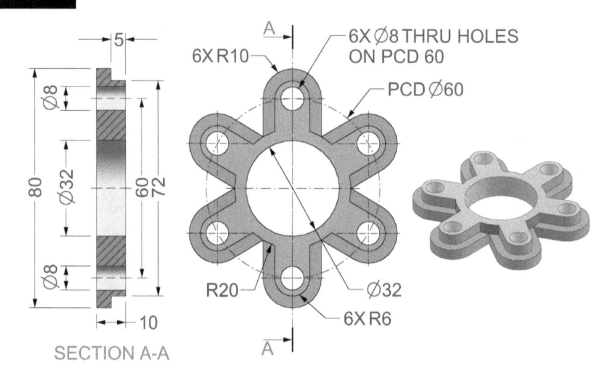

6X R10

6X Ø8 THRU HOLES
ON PCD 60

PCD Ø60

5

Ø8

Ø32

80

60

72

Ø8

10

R20

Ø32

6X R6

SECTION A-A

A

A

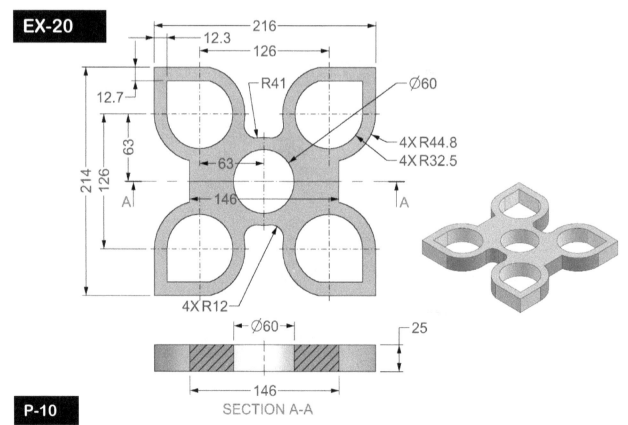

216

12.3

126

12.7

R41

Ø60

63

4X R44.8
4X R32.5

214

126

63

146

A

A

4X R12

Ø60

25

146

SECTION A-A

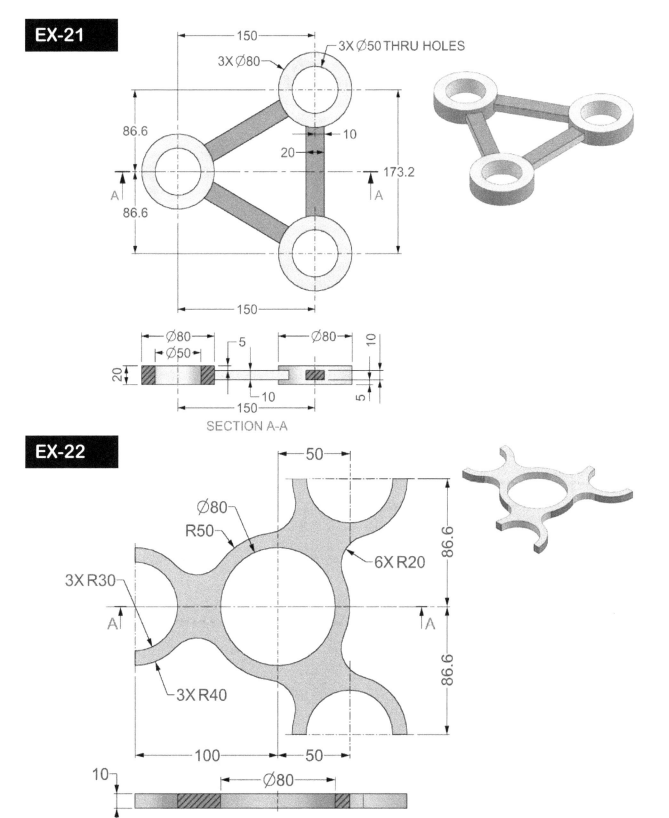

EX-21

150

3X Ø50 THRU HOLES

3X Ø80

86.6

86.6

173.2

A

A

10

20

150

SECTION A-A

Ø80
Ø50
20
150
5
10
Ø80
10
5

EX-22

50

Ø80

R50

6X R20

86.6

3X R30

A

A

86.6

3X R40

100

50

10

Ø80

SECTION A-A

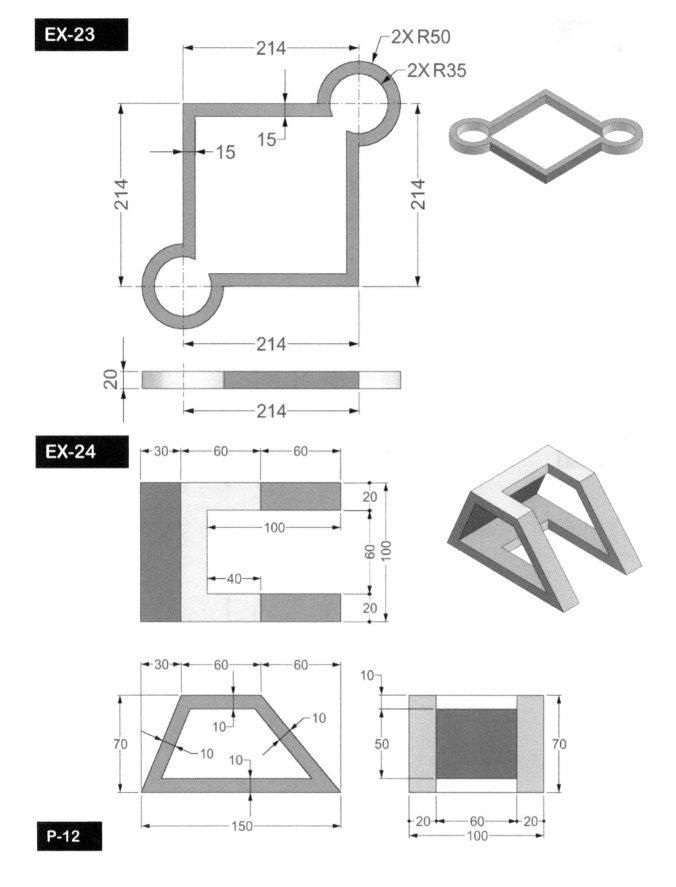

EX-23

2X R50
2X R35
214
15
15
214
214
214
20
214

EX-24

30
60
60
20
100
60
100
40
20

P-12

30
60
60
10
10
10
70
10
10
150
10
50
70
20
60
20
100

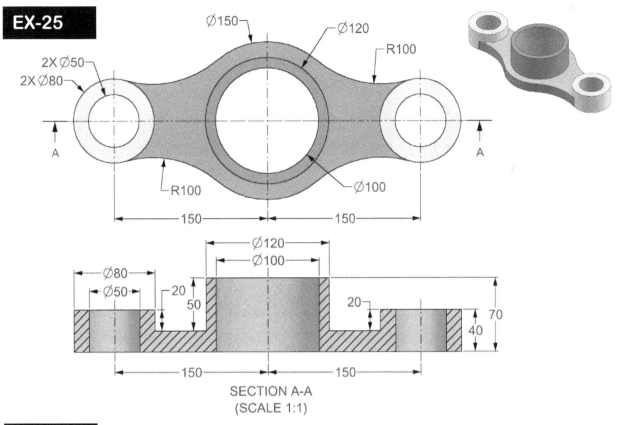

Ø150
Ø120
R100
2X Ø50
2X Ø80
R100
Ø100
150
150

Ø120
Ø100
Ø80
Ø50
20
50
20
70
40
150
150

SECTION A-A
(SCALE 1:1)

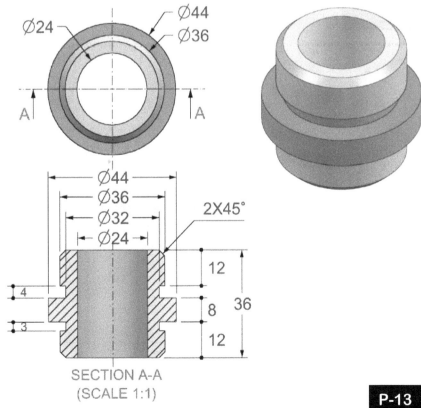

Ø24
Ø44
Ø36

A
A

Ø44
Ø36
Ø32
Ø24
2X45°
12
4
8
36
3
12

SECTION A-A
(SCALE 1:1)

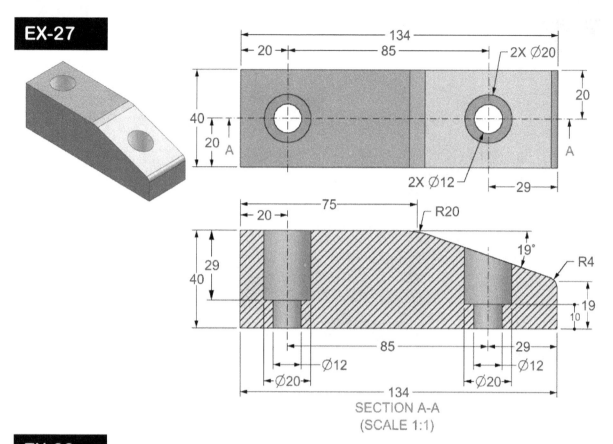

2X ∅20

2X ∅12

SECTION A-A
(SCALE 1:1)

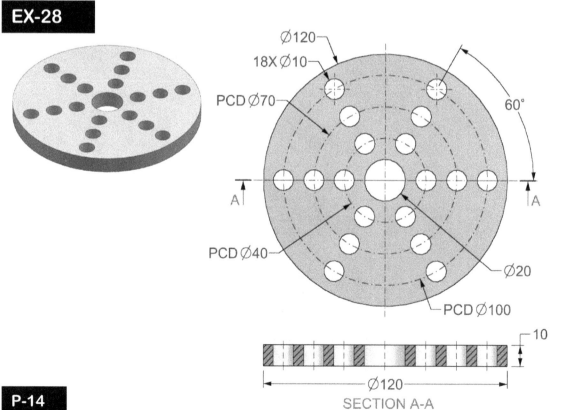

∅120

18X ∅10

PCD ∅70

60°

PCD ∅40

∅20

PCD ∅100

∅120

SECTION A-A

EX-29

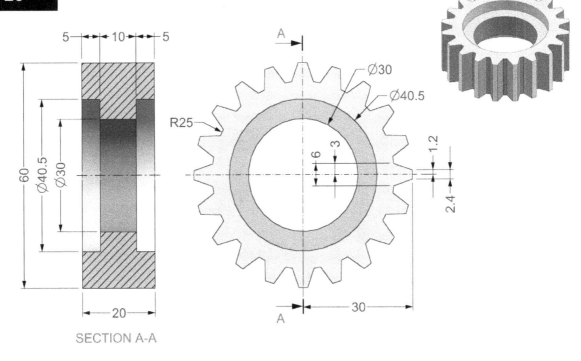

SECTION A-A

EX-30

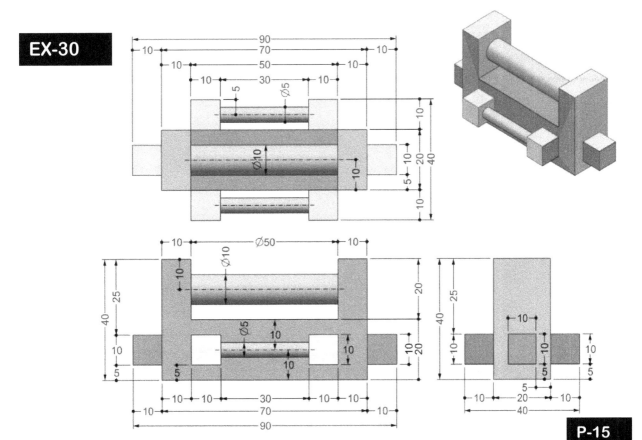

P-15

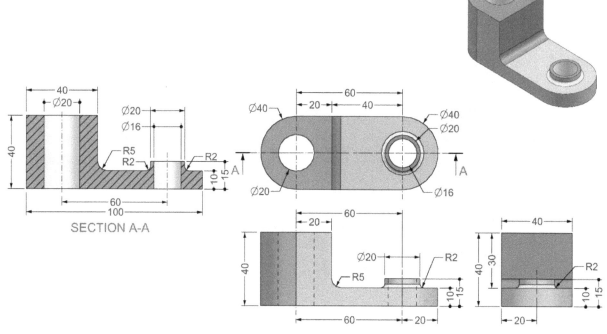

SECTION A-A

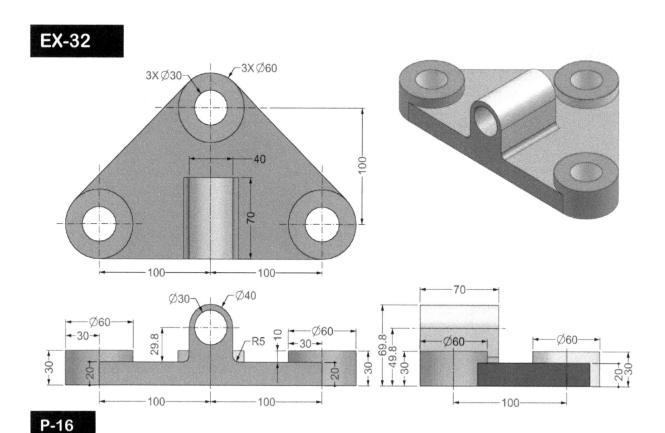

EX-33

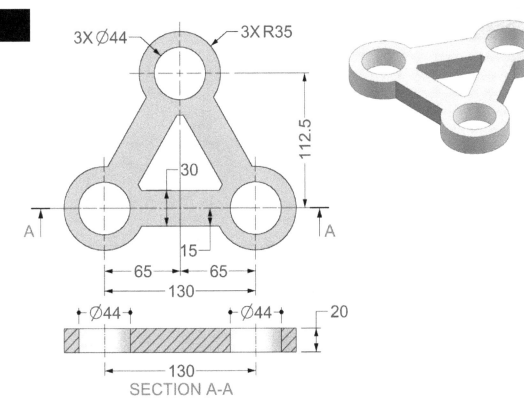

3X ⌀44   3X R35

112.5

30

15

65   65

130

⌀44   ⌀44   20

130

SECTION A-A

EX-34

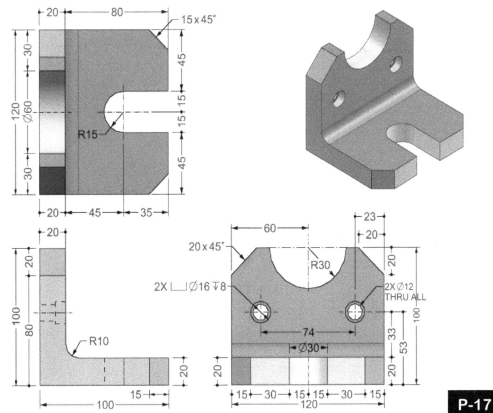

20   80   15 x 45°

30

45

45

120   ⌀60   15   15

R15

30   15

20   45   35

20

20

100   80

R10

100   15

20 x 45°   60   23   20

R30   20

2X ⌞ ⌀16 ↧8   2X ⌀12 THRU ALL

74   33   100

⌀30   53

20   20

15   30   15   15   30   15

120

P-17

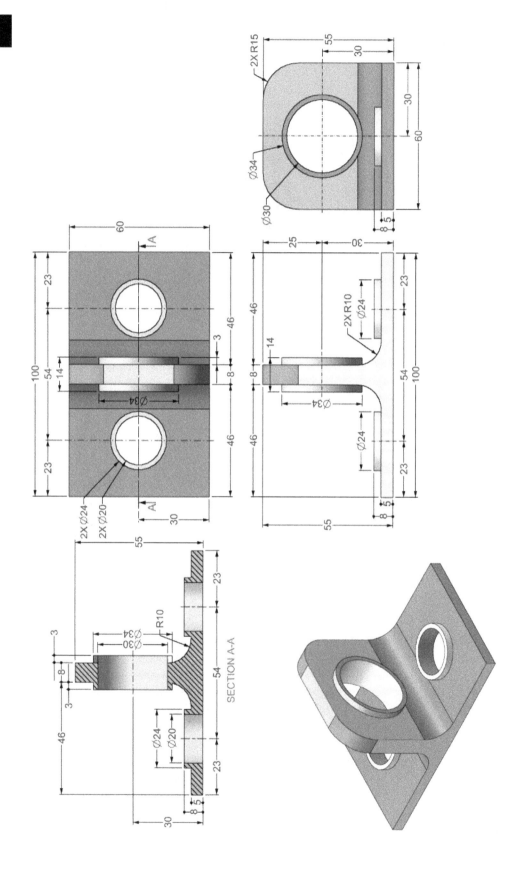

2X R15
55
30
30
60
Ø34
Ø30
8
5

60
A
23
46
3
100
54
14
8
Ø34
46
23
2X Ø24
2X Ø20
A
30

25
30
46
2X R10
Ø24
14
8
8
54
100
Ø34
46
Ø24
23
5
8
55

55
23
3
R10
Ø34
Ø30
8
3
54
46
Ø24
Ø20
23
5
8
30

SECTION A-A

EX-36

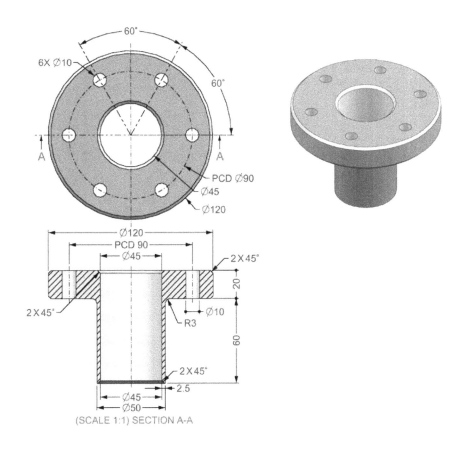

6X Ø10

60°

60°

PCD Ø90
Ø45
Ø120

Ø120
PCD 90
Ø45
2 X 45°
20
2 X 45°
Ø10
R3
60
2 X 45°
2.5
Ø45
Ø50
(SCALE 1:1) SECTION A-A

EX-37

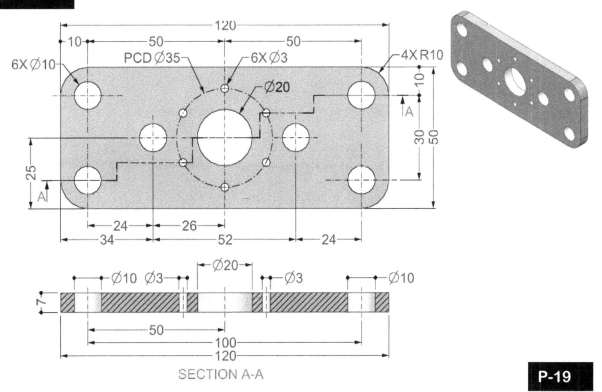

120
10
50
50
6X Ø10
PCD Ø35
6X Ø3
4X R10
Ø20
10
A
30
50
25
A
24
26
34
52
24

Ø20
Ø10 Ø3
Ø3
Ø10
7
50
100
120
SECTION A-A

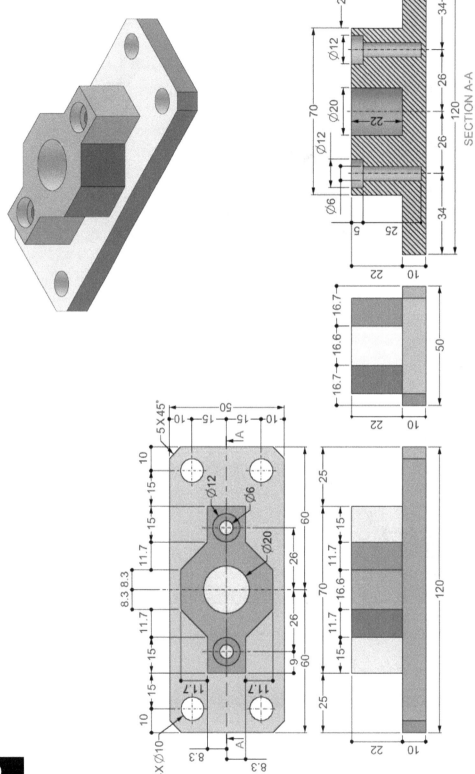

SECTION A-A

EX-39

70

R20
Ø20

40

45

R25
Ø20

45

20

30

10

10

45

65

A — A

20

2X R10

Ø40

Ø20

25

45

SECTION A-A

EX-40

Ø60

20

10

5

Ø50

Ø60

Ø50

5 — 10 — 5

30

Ø60

20

P-21

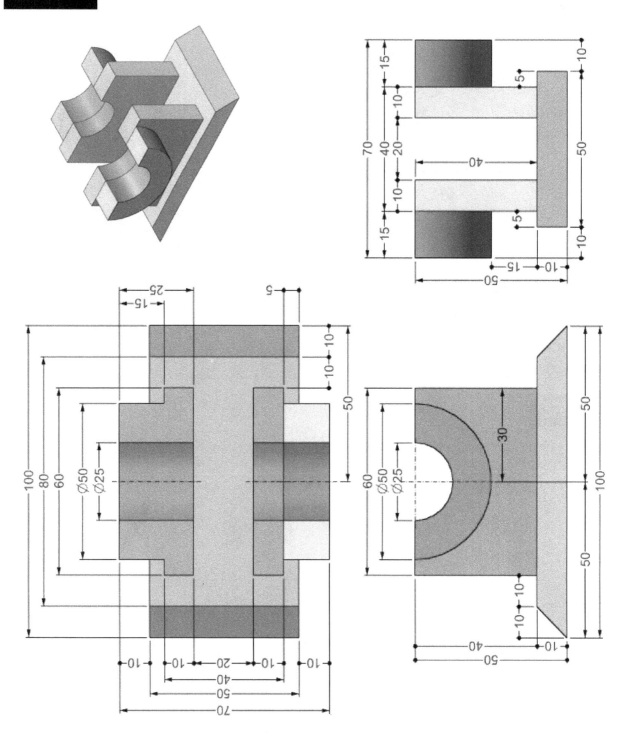

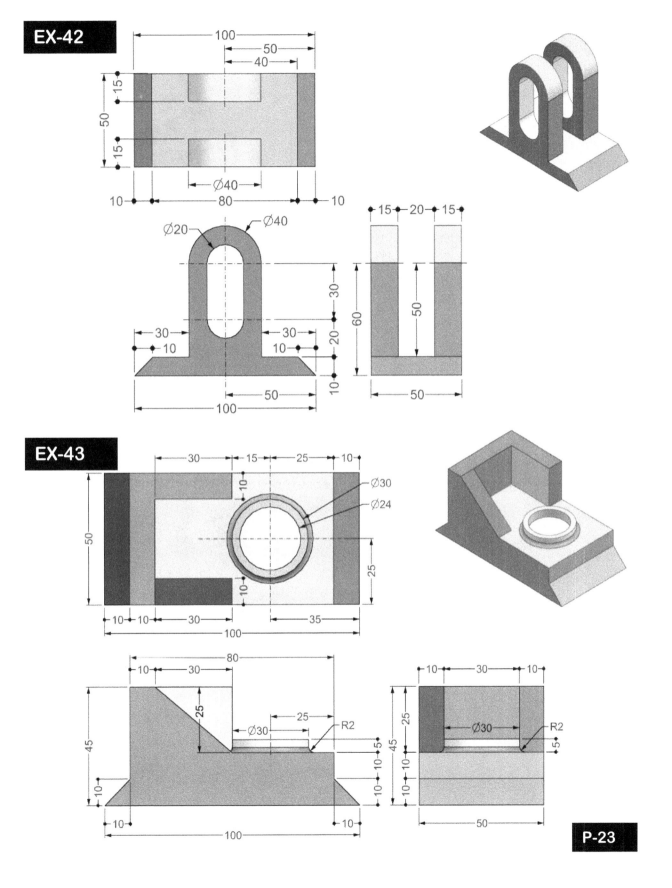

EX-42

EX-43

P-23

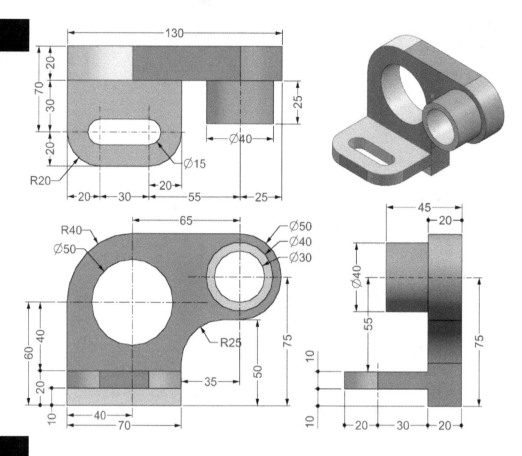

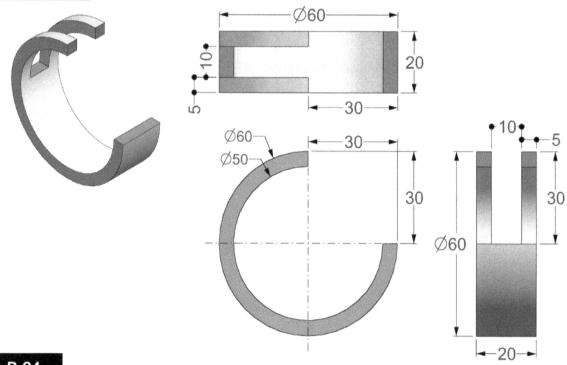

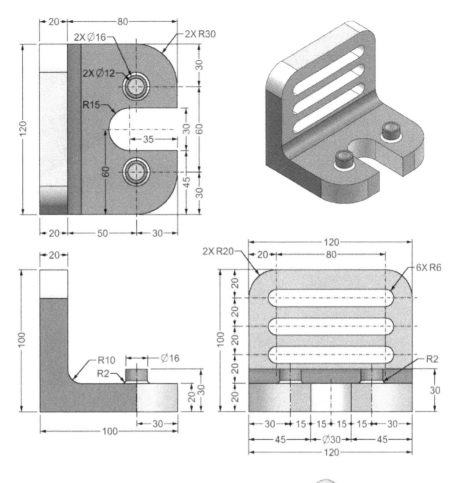

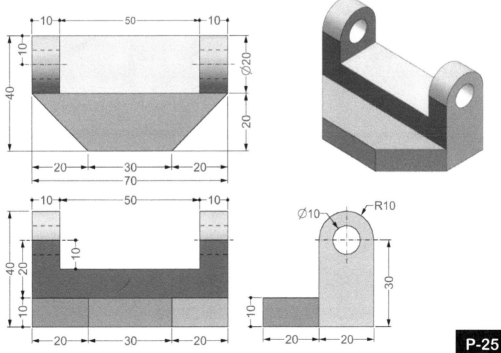

EX-48

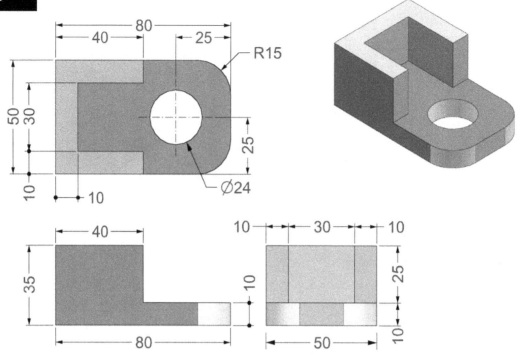

EX-49

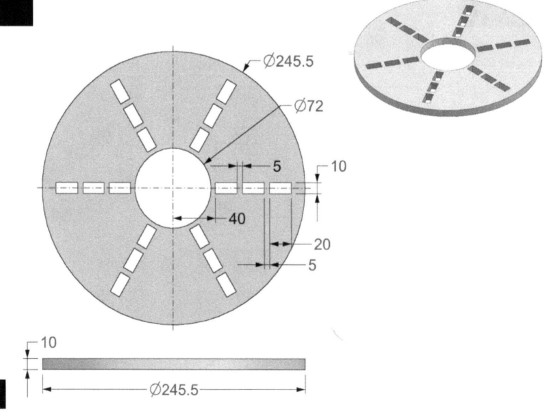

P-26

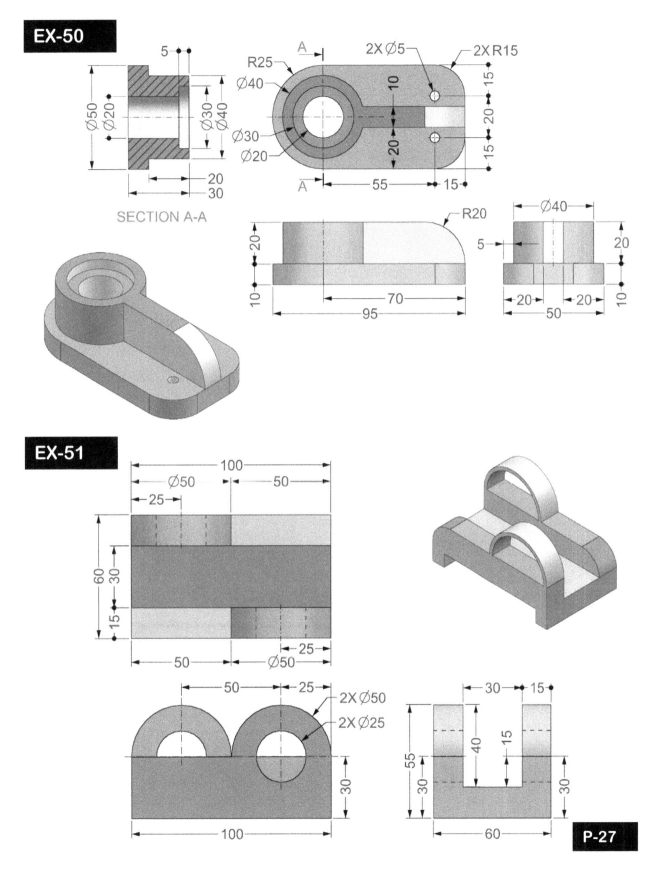

EX-50

5
Ø50
Ø20
Ø30
Ø40
20
30

SECTION A-A

A
R25
Ø40
Ø30
Ø20
2X Ø5
2X R15
10
15
20
15
20
55
15

R20
20
10
70
95

Ø40
5
20
20
50
10

EX-51

100
Ø50
50
25
60
30
15
50
Ø50
25

50
25
2X Ø50
2X Ø25
30
100

30
15
55
30
40
15
30
60

P-27

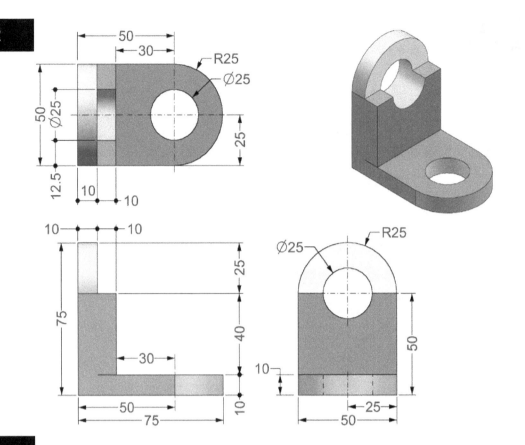

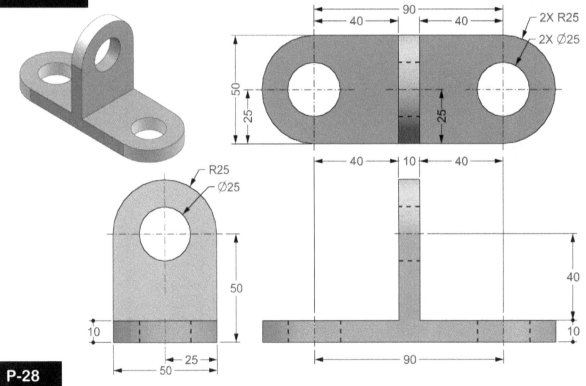

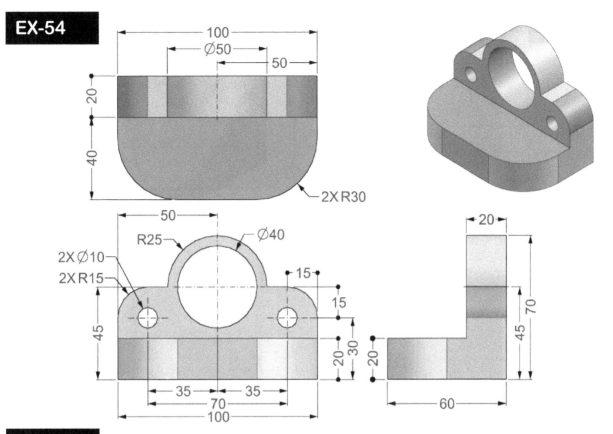

100
Ø50
50
20
40
2X R30

50
R25
Ø40
2X Ø10
2X R15
45
15
15
35   35
20   30
70
100
20
20
70
45
60

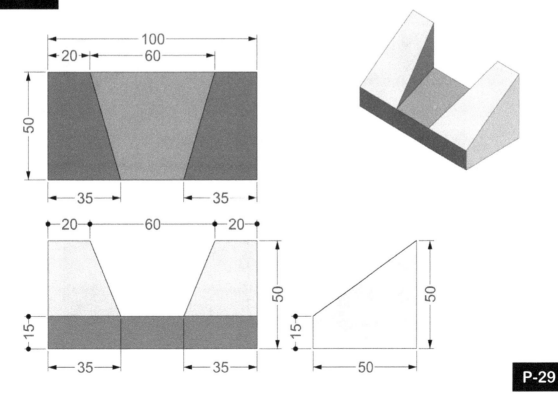

100
20   60
50
35   35

20   60   20
50
15
35   35

15
50
50

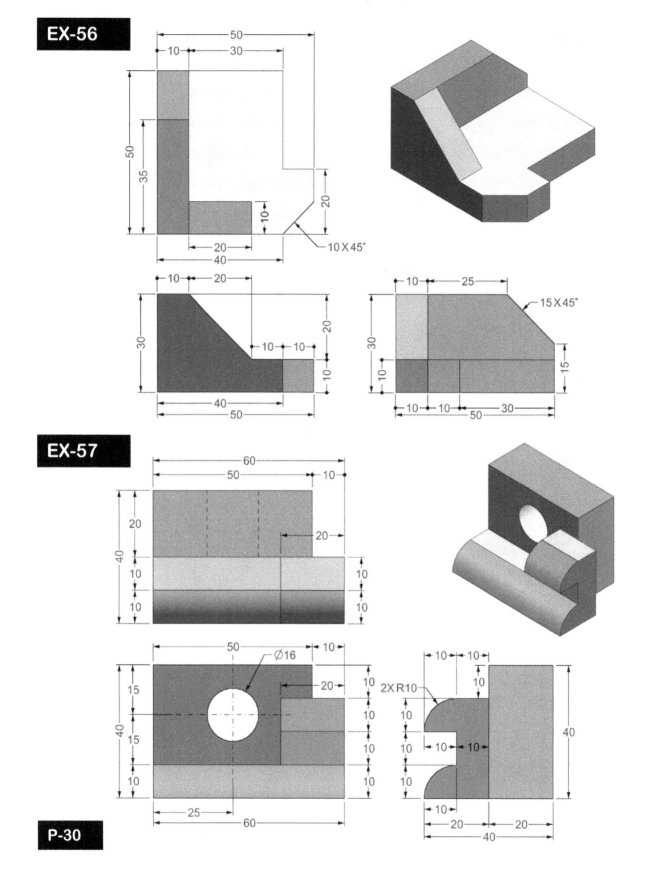

EX-56

50
10 30
50
35
20
10
20
40
10 X 45°

10 20
30
20
10 10
10
40
50

10 25
15 X 45°
30
10
15
10 10 30
50

EX-57

60
50 10
20
20
40
10 10
10 10

50 Ø16
10
15 20 10
10
40 10
15 10
2X R10 10 10
10 10 10
10 10
10 10
25 10 40
60 10 10
20 20
40

P-30

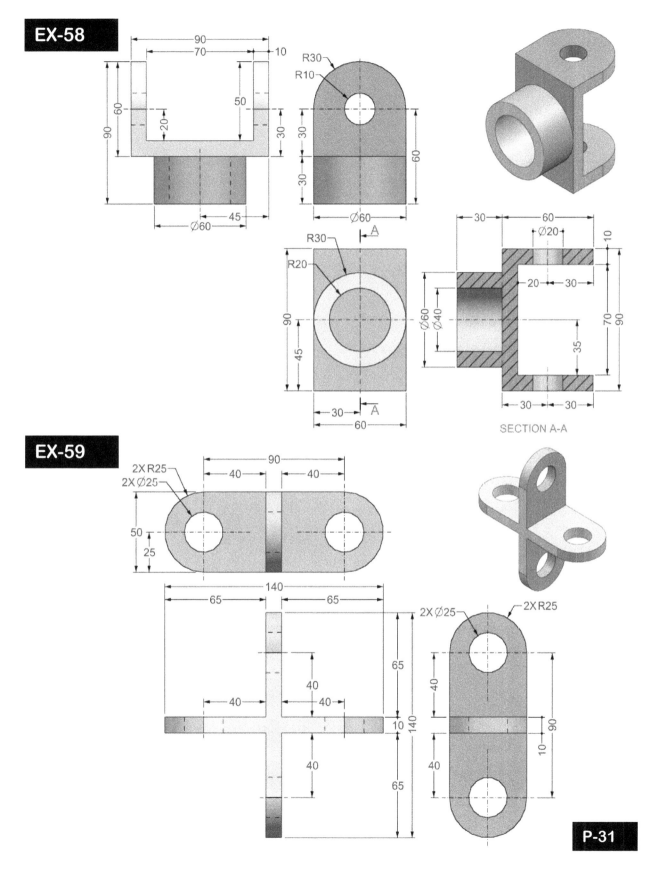

EX-58

R30
R10
90
90
70
10
60
50
20
30
45
Ø60
Ø60

R30
R20
90
45
30
60
30
A

R30
R10
30
30
60
Ø60
A

30
60
Ø20
10
20
30
Ø60
Ø40
70
90
35
30
30

SECTION A-A

EX-59

2X R25
2X Ø25
90
40
40
50
25

140
65
65
65
40
40
140
10
40
65

2X Ø25
2X R25
40
40
90
10
40

P-31

EX-60

Ø50
22.5 — 2X Ø10
15
25
60
43.9
10
25
15
50
45
95

Ø50
Ø40
R4 R10
10
R10
40
155
130
10
45 45
R10
R10
55
30
10 10
22.5 22.5
100
140
80
40

60
85.4
100
155
34.6
10 25
40
60

EX-61

Ø120
20
50
R3
Ø50
10 10
R2
Ø50
Ø70

14 14
PCD Ø90
Ø70
Ø50
66
14
132
14
A
66
R60
Ø30
6X Ø10
66 66
132

132
Ø70
Ø50
Ø30
Ø10
10 10 10
R2
Ø50
Ø30
Ø10
R3
45 45
90
Ø120
10
100
50
20

Ø120
PCD Ø90
6X Ø10
ON PCD 90
Ø30
66
132
14
14
66
14 14
66 66
132

SECTION A-A

P-32

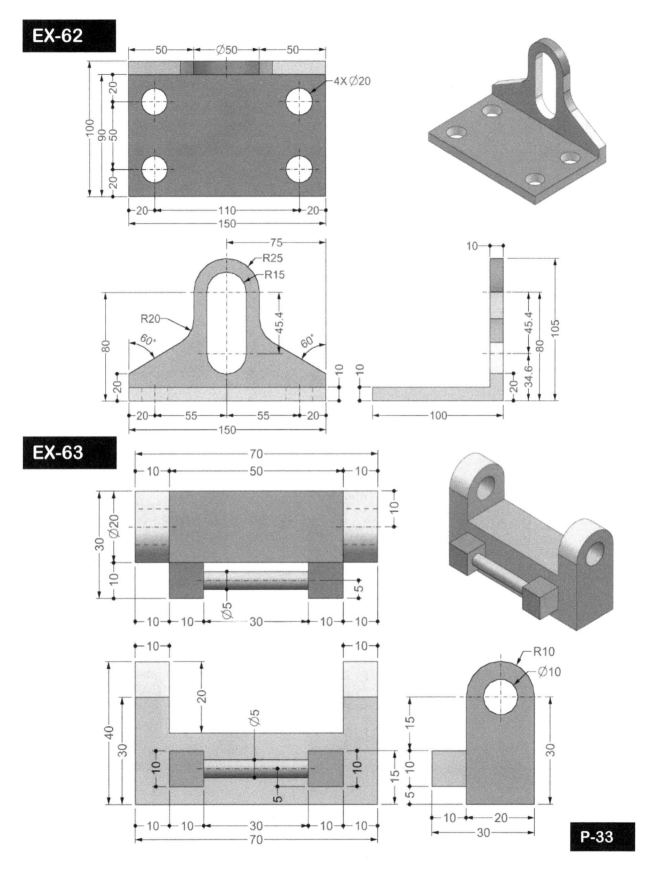

EX-62

EX-63

P-33

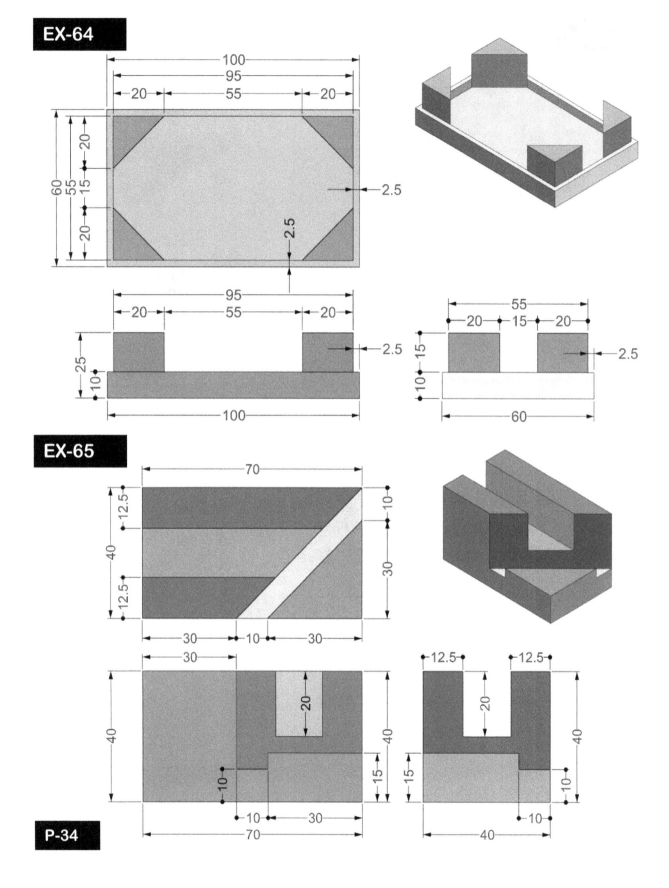

EX-64

EX-65

P-34

EX-66

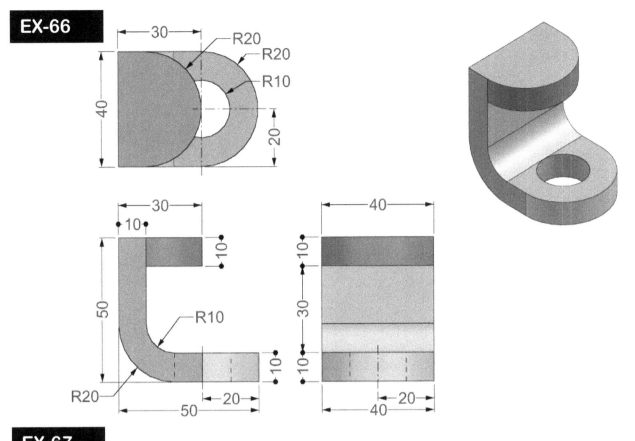

EX-67

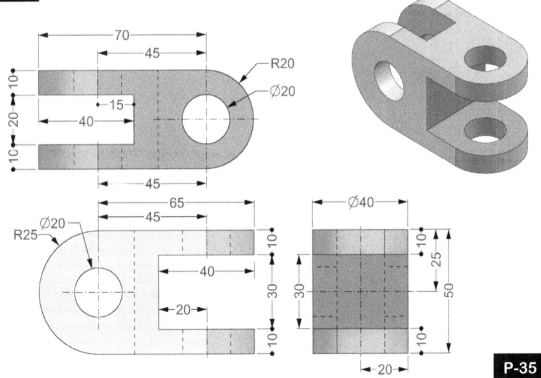

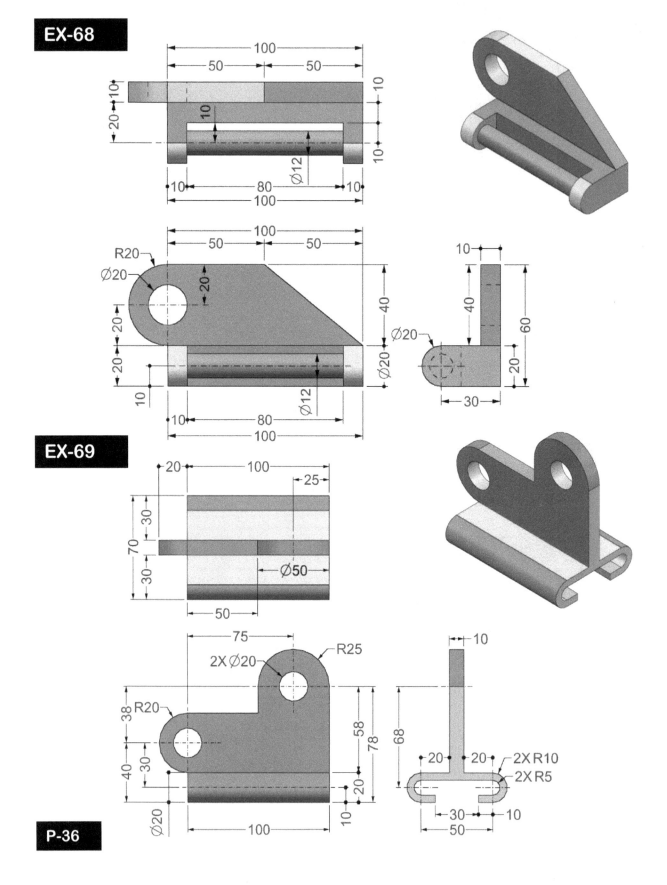

EX-68

EX-69

P-36

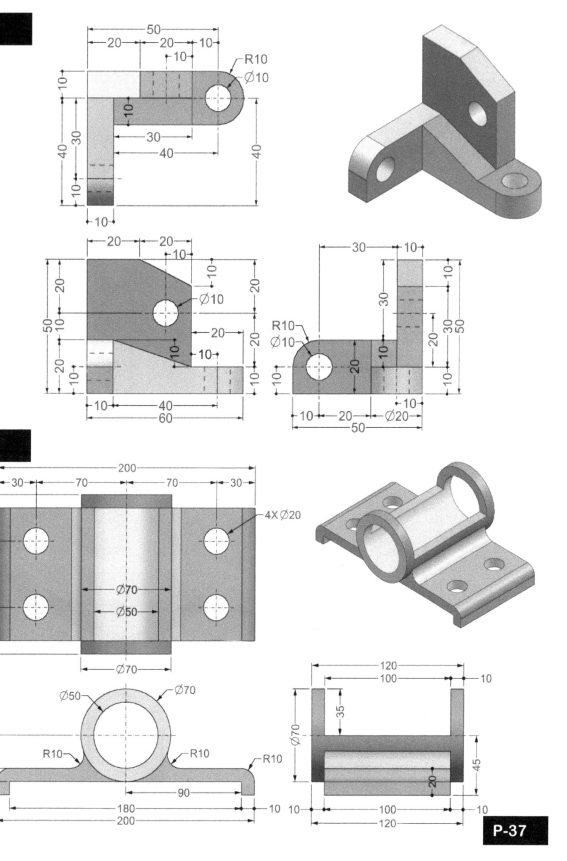

EX-70

EX-71

P-37

EX-72

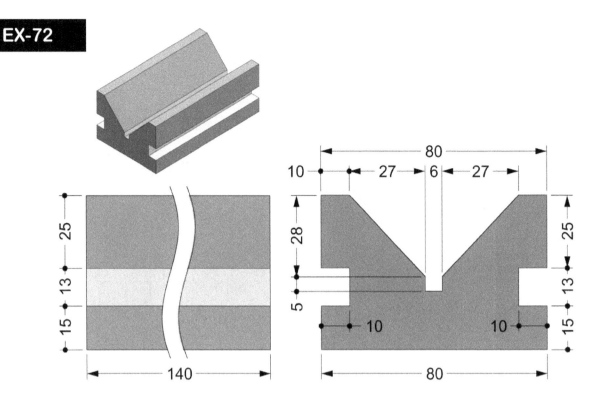

EX-73

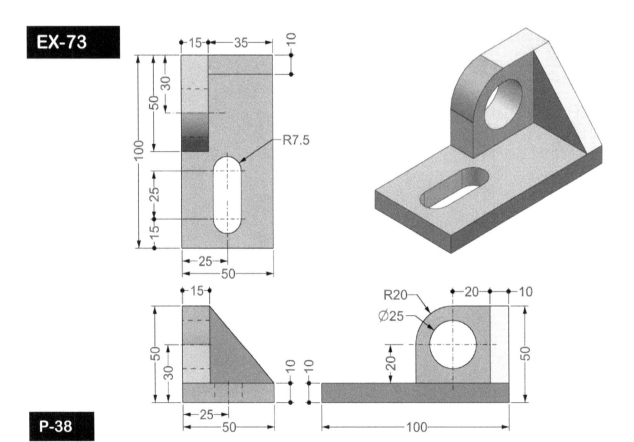

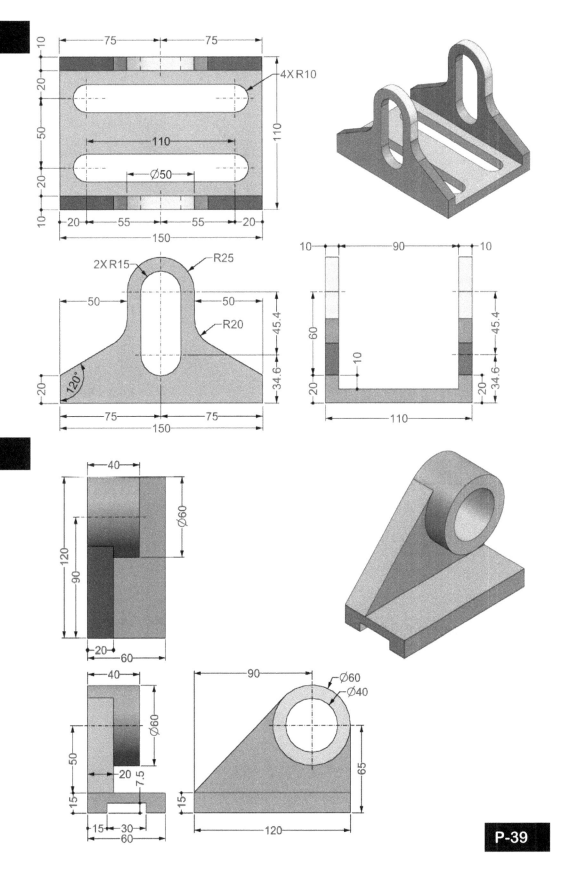

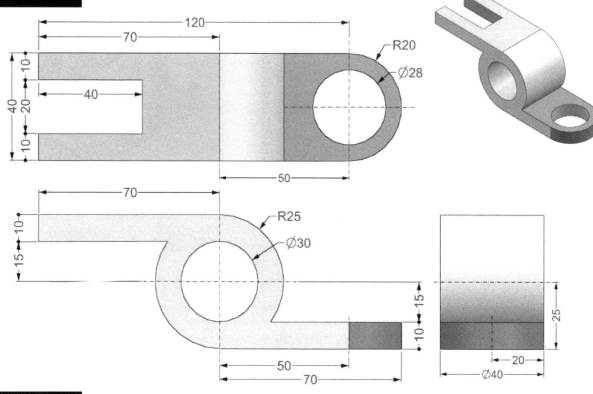

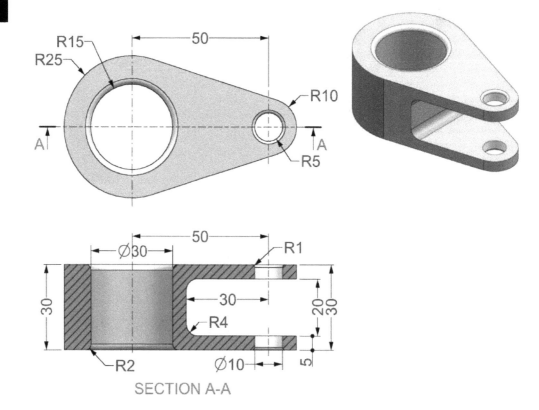

SECTION A-A

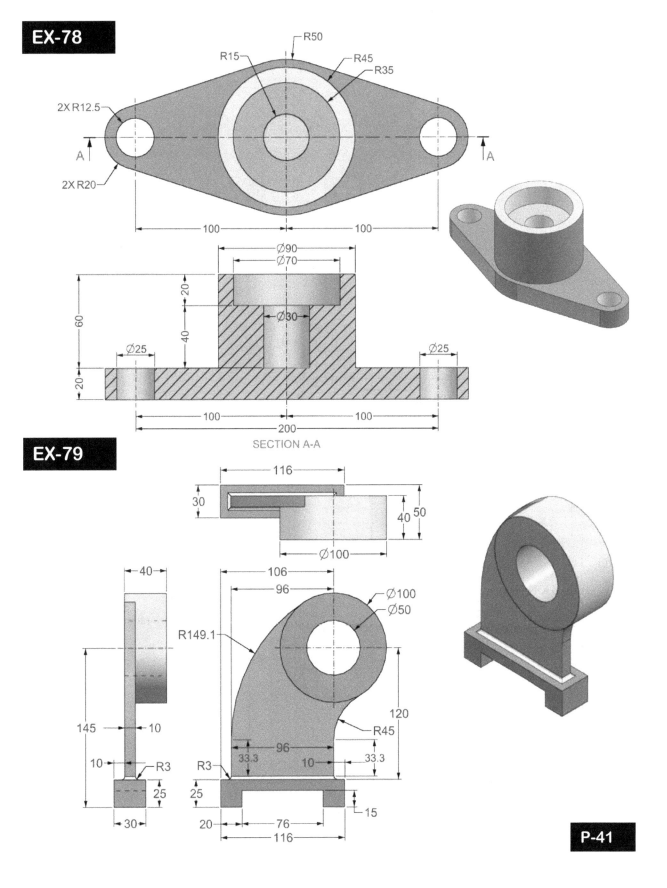

EX-78

R50
R15
R45
R35
2X R12.5
A
A
2X R20
100
100

Ø90
Ø70
20
40
Ø30
60
Ø25
Ø25
20
100
100
200
SECTION A-A

EX-79

116
30
40
50
Ø100

40
106
96
Ø100
Ø50
R149.1
120
R45
145
10
96
33.3
10
33.3
10
R3
R3
25
25
30
15
20
76
116

P-41

EX-80

6 HOLES, Ø10
ON DIA 32 PCD

4 HOLES, Ø8.6
ON DIA 54 PCD

Ø70

Ø16

A

A

Ø54

Ø32

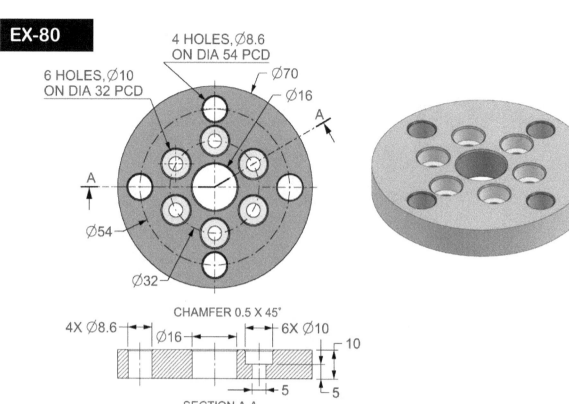

CHAMFER 0.5 X 45°

4X Ø8.6

Ø16

6X Ø10

10

5

5

SECTION A-A
(SCALE 1:1)

EX-81

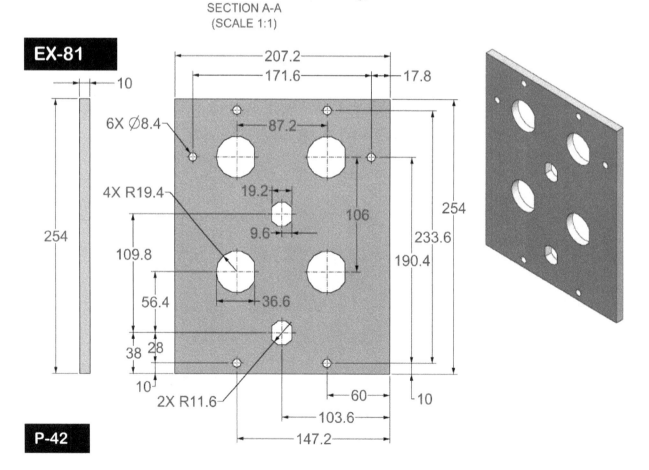

207.2

171.6

17.8

6X Ø8.4

87.2

254

4X R19.4

19.2

106

254

9.6

233.6

109.8

190.4

56.4

36.6

38 28

10

2X R11.6

60

10

103.6

147.2

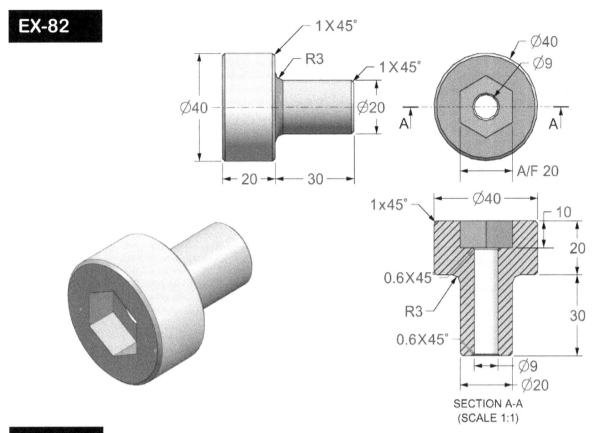

1 X 45°
R3
1 X 45°
Ø40
Ø40
Ø9
Ø20
20
30
A
A
A/F 20

1x45°
Ø40
10
20
0.6X45°
R3
30
0.6X45°
Ø9
Ø20

SECTION A-A
(SCALE 1:1)

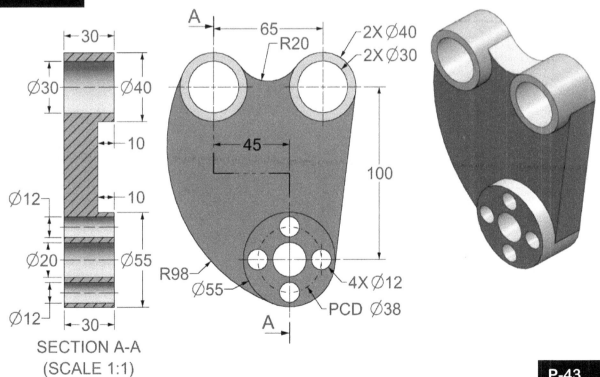

30
Ø30
Ø40
10
10
Ø12
Ø20
Ø55
Ø12
30

SECTION A-A
(SCALE 1:1)

A
65
R20
2X Ø40
2X Ø30
45
100
R98
Ø55
4X Ø12
PCD Ø38
A

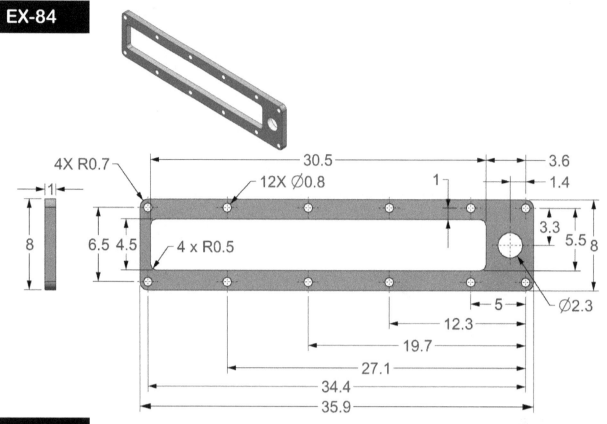

4X R0.7

12X Ø0.8

4 x R0.5

30.5

3.6

1.4

1

3.3

5.5

8

Ø2.3

5

12.3

19.7

27.1

34.4

35.9

1

8

6.5 4.5

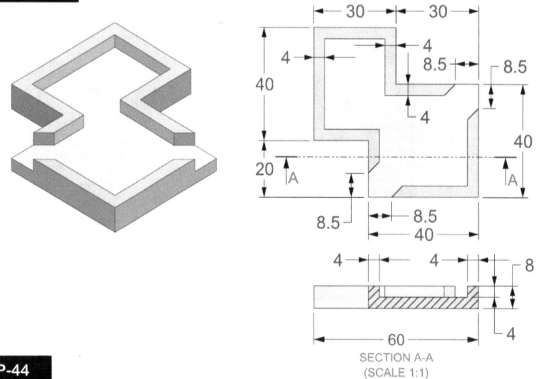

30

30

4

4

8.5

8.5

40

4

4

40

20

A

A

8.5

8.5

40

4

4

8

60

4

SECTION A-A
(SCALE 1:1)

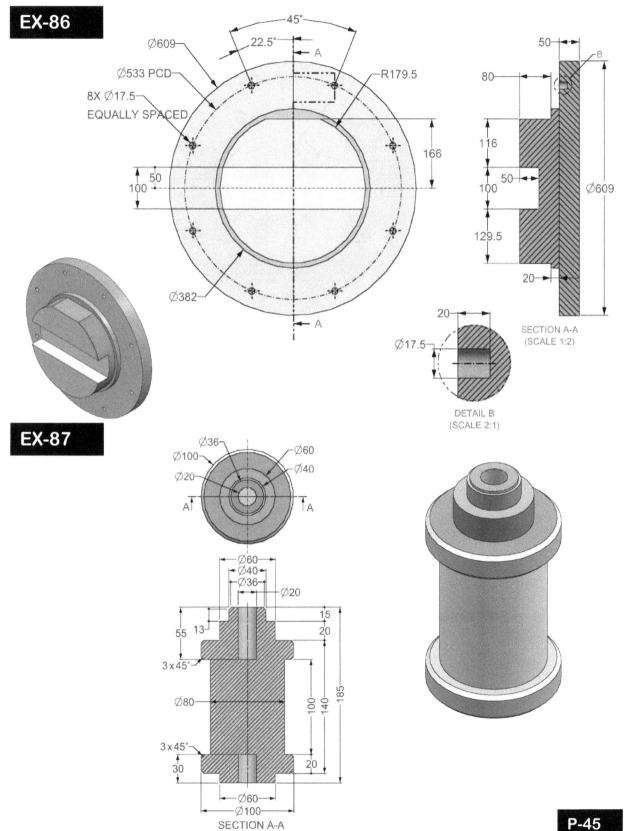

EX-86

⌀609
⌀533 PCD
8X ⌀17.5
EQUALLY SPACED
45°
22.5°
A
R179.5
166
50
100
⌀382
A

50
80
B
116
50
100
129.5
20
⌀609

SECTION A-A
(SCALE 1:2)

20
⌀17.5

DETAIL B
(SCALE 2:1)

EX-87

⌀36
⌀100
⌀60
⌀20
⌀40
A   A

⌀60
⌀40
⌀36
⌀20
15
20
55
13
3 x 45°
100
140
185
⌀80
3 x 45°
30
20
⌀60
⌀100

SECTION A-A

P-45

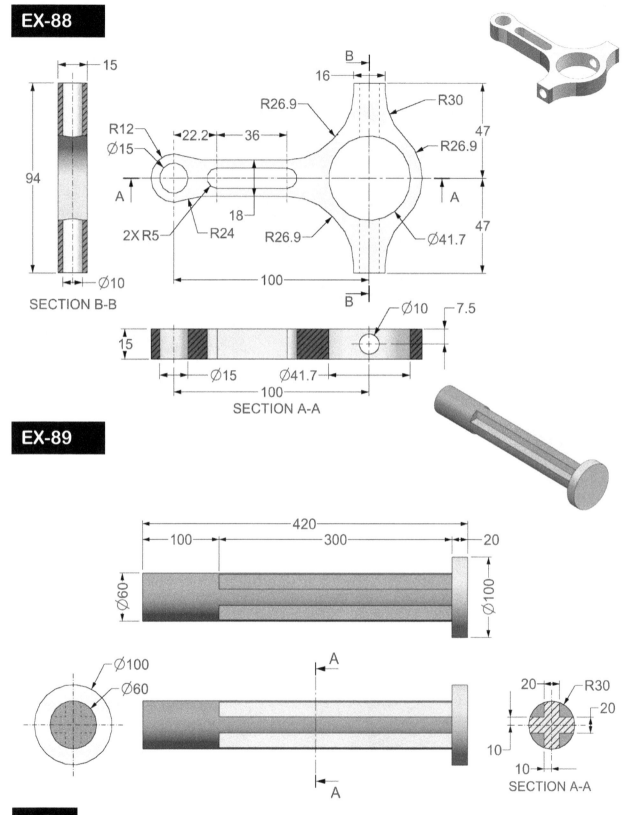

EX-88

15

94

R12
Ø15

22.2   36

R26.9

16

B

R30

47

R26.9

47

A

2X R5   R24

18

R26.9

Ø41.7

100

B

SECTION B-B

Ø10

15

Ø15   Ø41.7

100

Ø10   7.5

SECTION A-A

EX-89

420

100   300   20

Ø60   Ø100

Ø100
Ø60

A

A

20   R30

20

10

10

SECTION A-A

P-46

EX-90

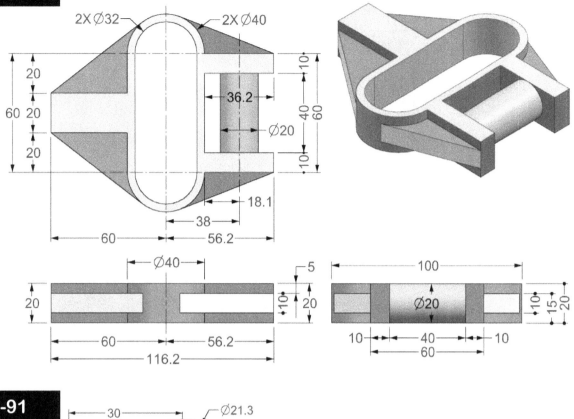

2X ∅32 2X ∅40

20
60 20
20

10
40 60
10

36.2
∅20

18.1
38
56.2
60

∅40
20
60 56.2
116.2

5
10 20

100
∅20
10 40 10
60
10 15 20

EX-91

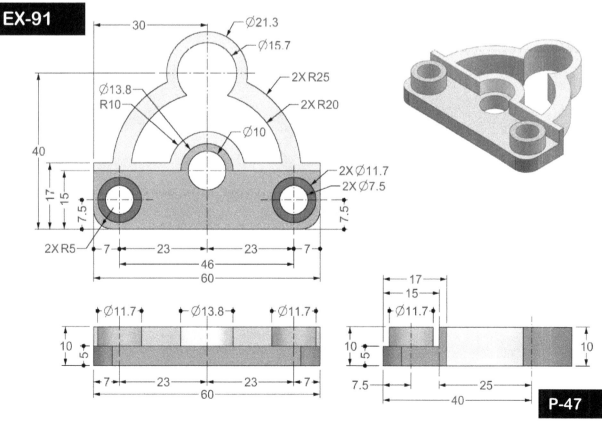

30
∅21.3
∅15.7
2X R25
∅13.8
R10
2X R20
∅10
40
17
15
7.5
2X ∅11.7
2X ∅7.5
2X R5
7 23 23 7
46
60
7.5

∅11.7 ∅13.8 ∅11.7
10
5
7 23 23 7
60

17
15
∅11.7
10
5
7.5 25
40
10

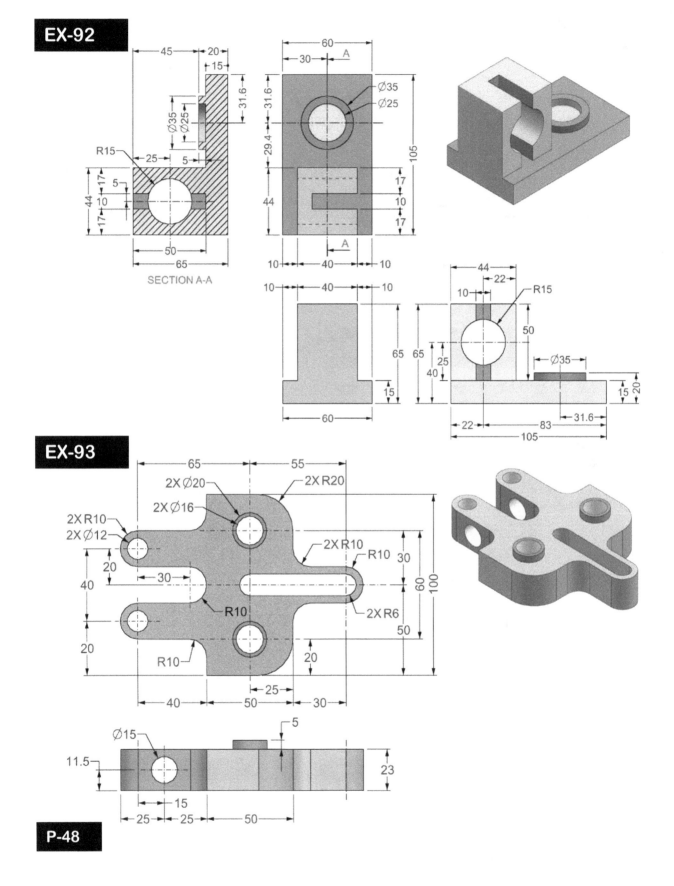

EX-92

SECTION A-A

EX-93

P-48

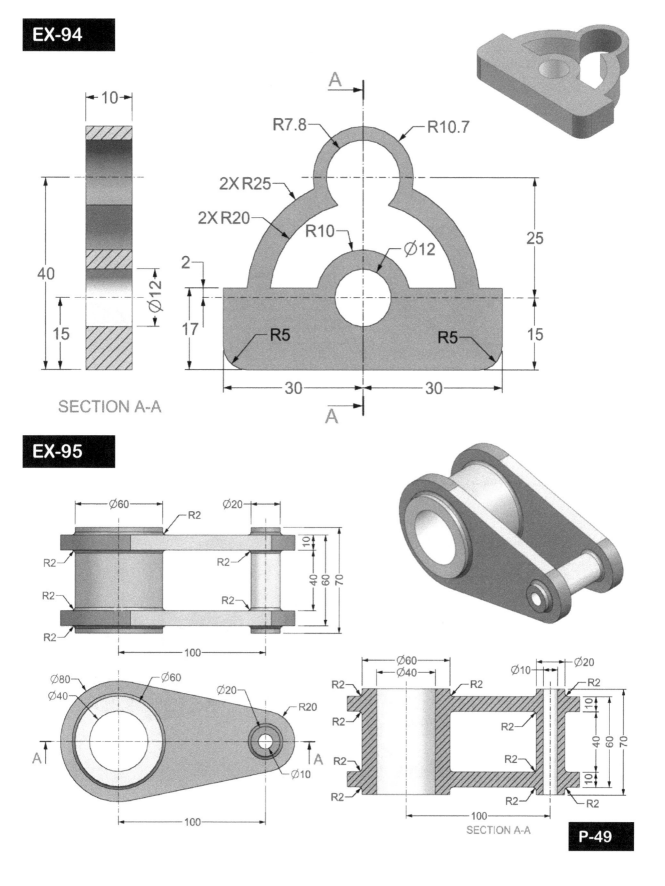

EX-94

10

R7.8   R10.7

2X R25

2X R20   R10   Ø12

40   Ø12   2   25

17   15

R5   R5

15

30   30

A

SECTION A-A

EX-95

Ø60   R2   Ø20

R2   R2   10

R2   R2   40   60   70

R2   R2

100

Ø80   Ø60   Ø20

Ø40   R20

A   A

Ø10

100

Ø60   Ø10   Ø20

Ø40

R2   R2   R2

R2   10

R2   R2   40   60   70

R2   R2   10

R2   R2   R2

100

SECTION A-A

P-49

EX-96

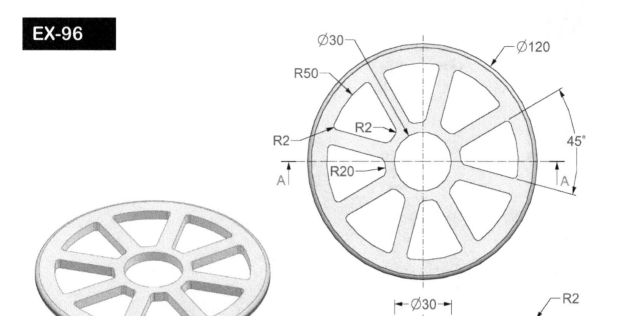

Ø30
Ø120
R50
R2
R2
45°
R2
R20
A
A

Ø30
Ø120
R2
R2
SECTION A-A

EX-97

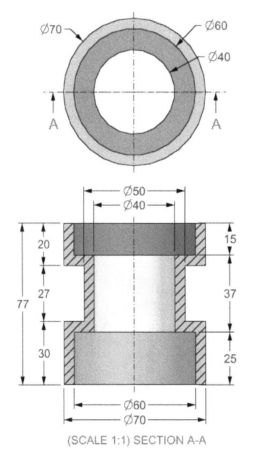
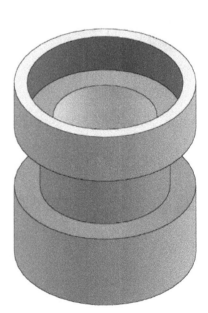

Ø70
Ø60
Ø40
A
A

Ø50
Ø40
20
15
27
37
77
30
25
Ø60
Ø70

(SCALE 1:1) SECTION A-A

P-50

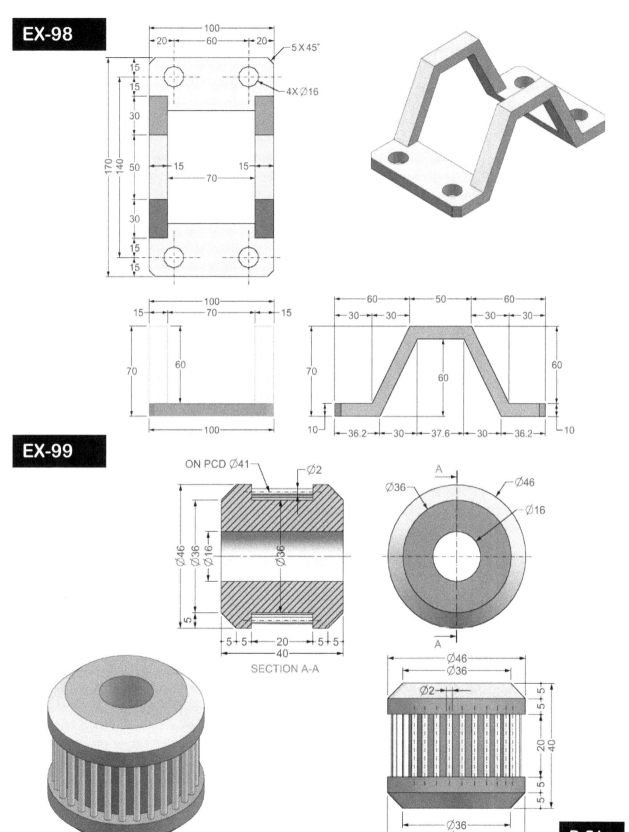

EX-98

5 X 45°
4X Ø16

EX-99

ON PCD Ø41
Ø2
SECTION A-A

A
Ø36
Ø46
Ø16
A

Ø46
Ø36
Ø2
Ø36
Ø46

P-51

EX-100

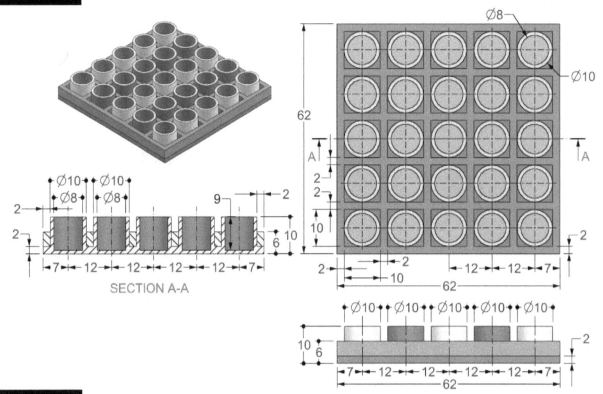

SECTION A-A

EX-101

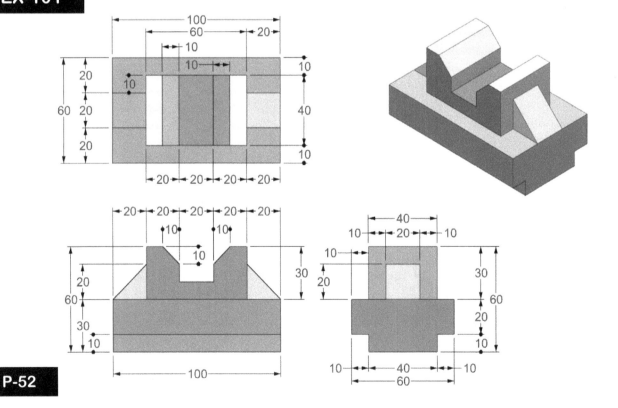

P-52

EX-102

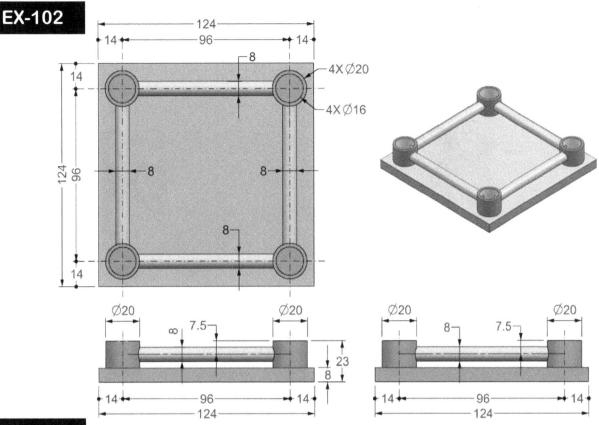

EX-103

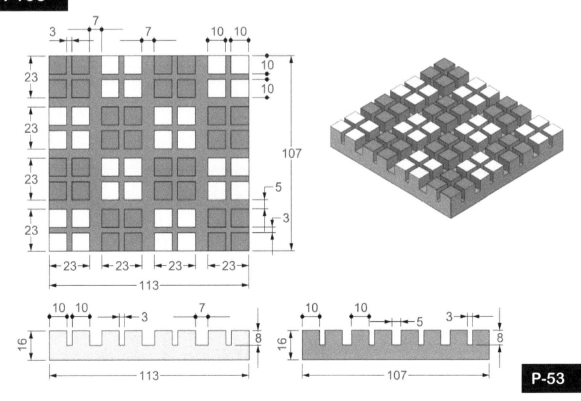

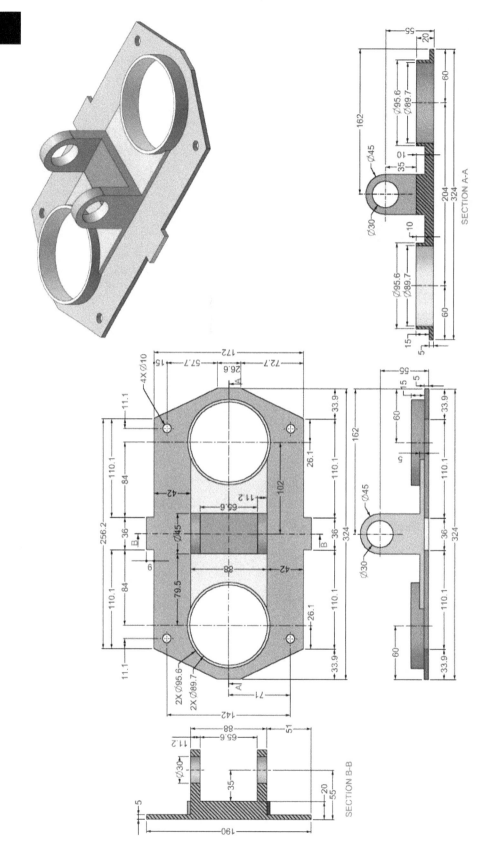

SECTION A-A

SECTION B-B

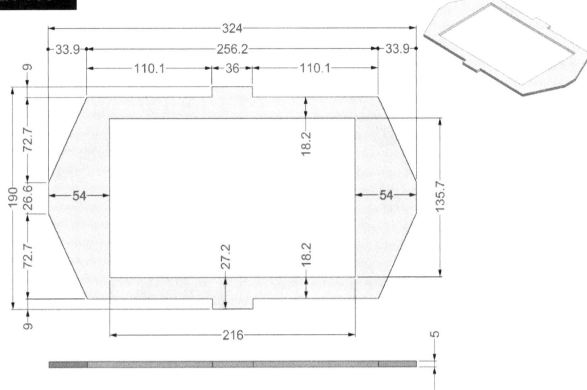

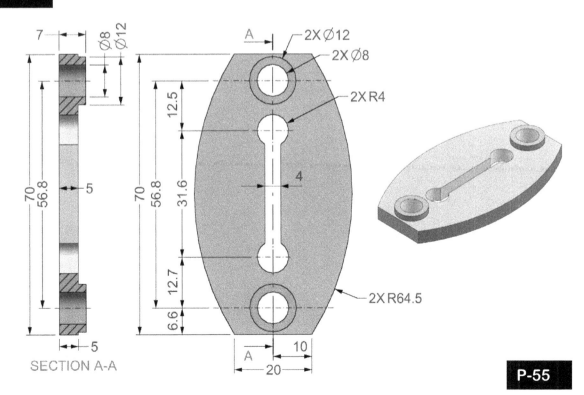

SECTION A-A

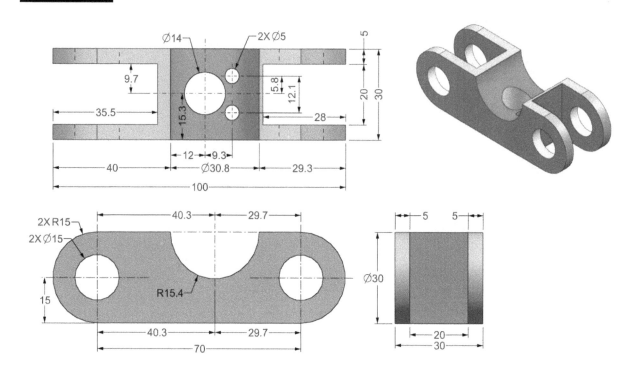

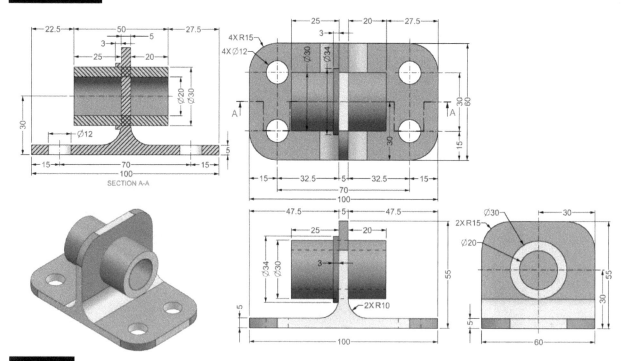

SECTION A-A

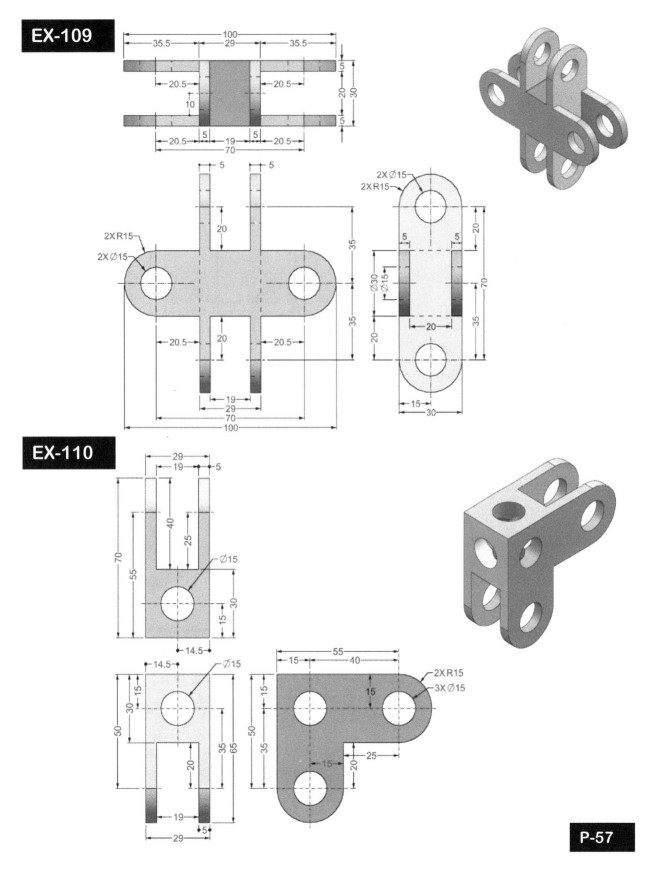

EX-109

EX-110

EX-111

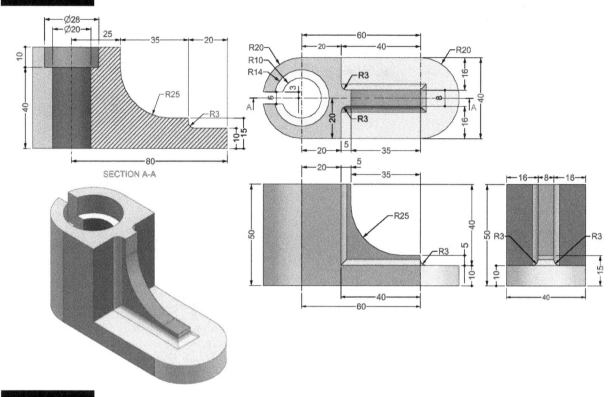

SECTION A-A

EX-112

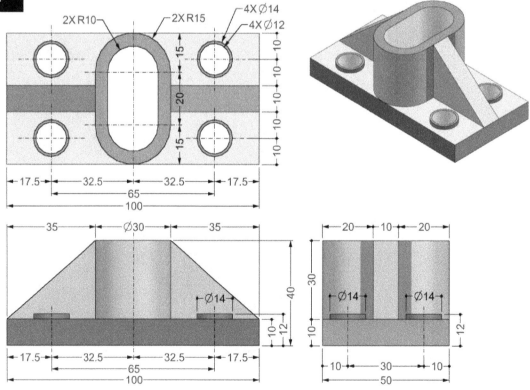

P-58

EX-113

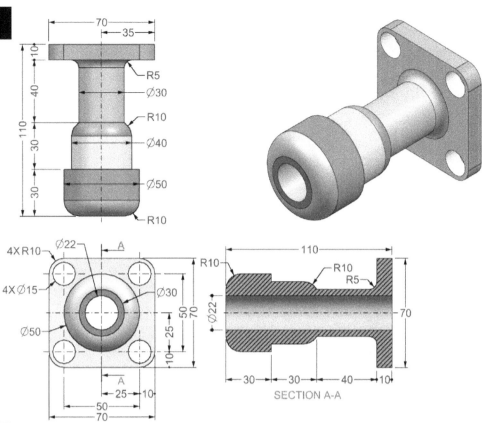

4X R10
4X Ø15
Ø50
Ø22
Ø30
Ø30
70
50
25
10
50
70
25
10
A
A

110
R10
R10
R5
Ø22
70
30
30
40
10

SECTION A-A

70
35
10
40
110
30
30
R5
Ø30
R10
Ø40
Ø50
R10

EX-114

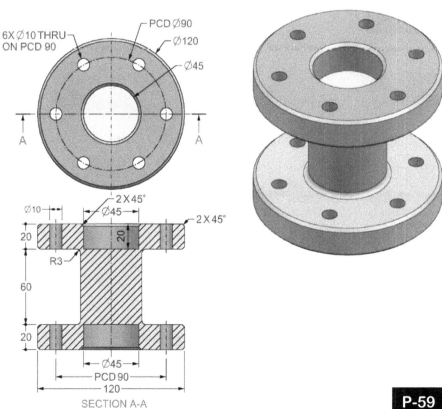

6X Ø10 THRU
ON PCD 90
PCD Ø90
Ø120
Ø45

A
A

2 X 45°
Ø10
Ø45
2 X 45°
20
20
R3
60
20
Ø45
PCD 90
120

SECTION A-A

EX-115

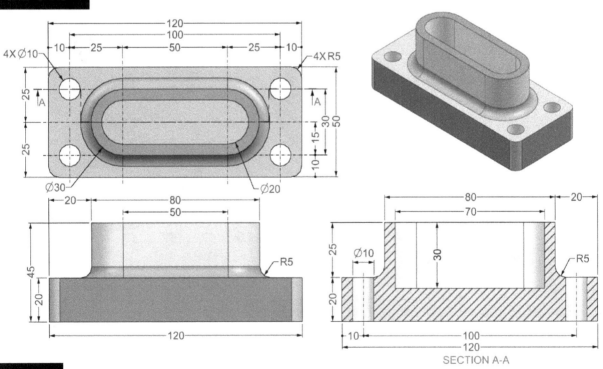

Ø120
6X Ø10
6X Ø8
PCD Ø90
Ø68
Ø45

Ø120
Ø68
R2
Ø10
10
10
20
120
60
20
10
PCD 90

Ø120
PCD 90
Ø68
Ø45
Ø10
40
2 X 45°
20
20
R3
60
R3
20
Ø8
Ø55
Ø50
Ø45
Ø8
SECTION A-A

EX-116

120
100
10
25
50
25
10
4X Ø10
4X R5
25
25
30
50
15
10
Ø30
Ø20

20
80
50
45
20
R5
120

80
70
20
25
Ø10
30
R5
10
100
120
SECTION A-A

P-60

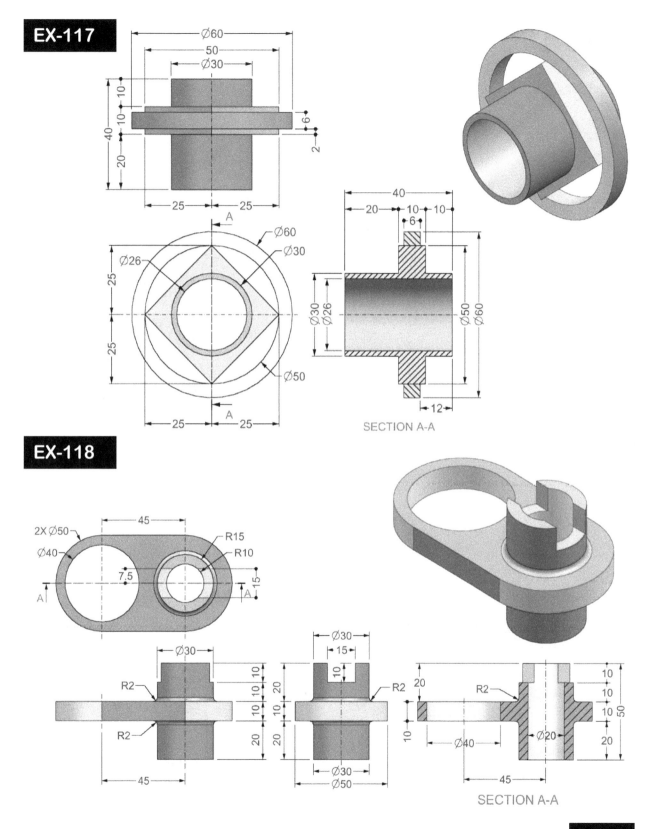

EX-117

Ø60
50
Ø30
40
10
10
20
6
2
25 25

A

Ø60
Ø30
Ø26
25
25
Ø50
25 25
A

40
20 10 10
6
Ø30 Ø26
Ø50 Ø60
12

SECTION A-A

EX-118

45
2X Ø50
Ø40
R15
R10
7.5
15
A A

Ø30
R2
R2
10 10 10 10
20
20
45

Ø30
15
10
20
10
20
R2
Ø30
Ø50

Ø30
20
R2
10
Ø40
Ø20
45
10 10 10 20
50

SECTION A-A

P-61

EX-119

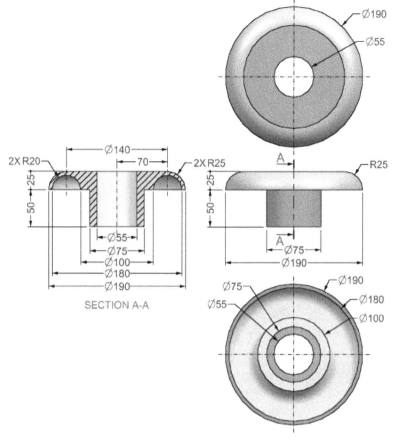

Ø140
70
2X R20
2X R25
25
50
Ø55
Ø75
Ø100
Ø180
Ø190

SECTION A-A

Ø190
Ø55
A
R25
25
50
Ø75
Ø190

A

Ø75
Ø190
Ø55
Ø180
Ø100

EX-120

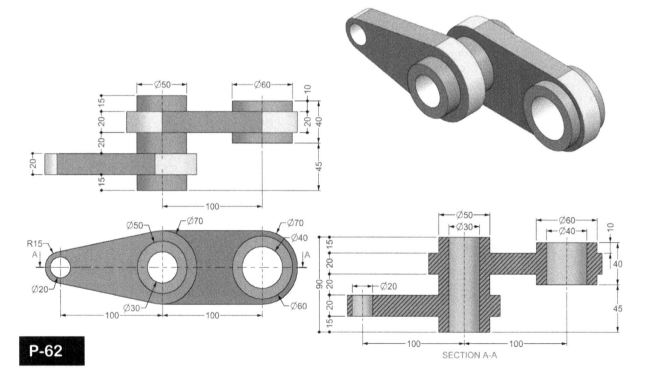

Ø50
Ø60
10
15
20
20
20
40
20
20
15
45
100

R15
A
Ø50
Ø70
Ø70
Ø40
Ø20
Ø60
Ø30
100
100
A

Ø50
Ø30
Ø60
Ø40
10
15
20
20
20
40
20
Ø20
90
45
15
100
100

SECTION A-A

P-62

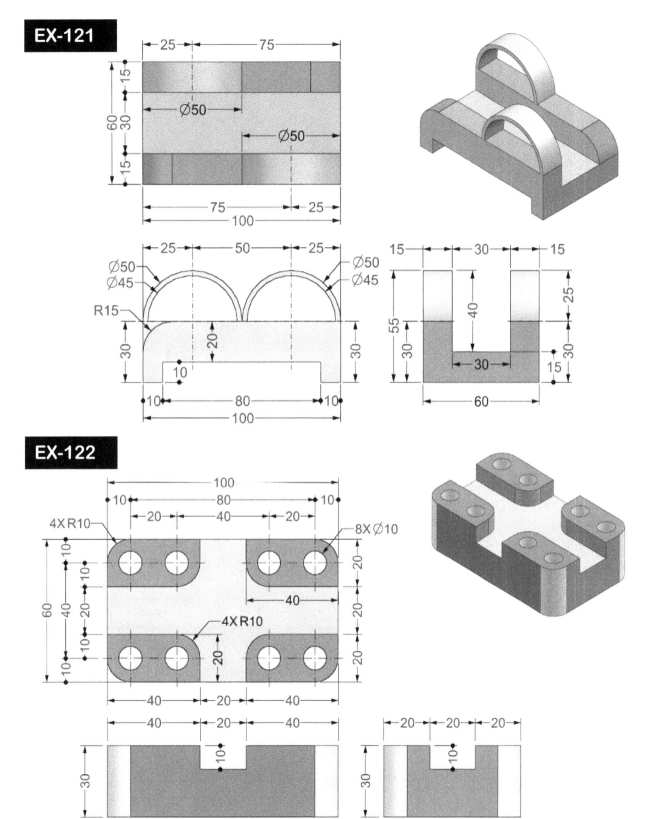

EX-121

EX-122

EX-123

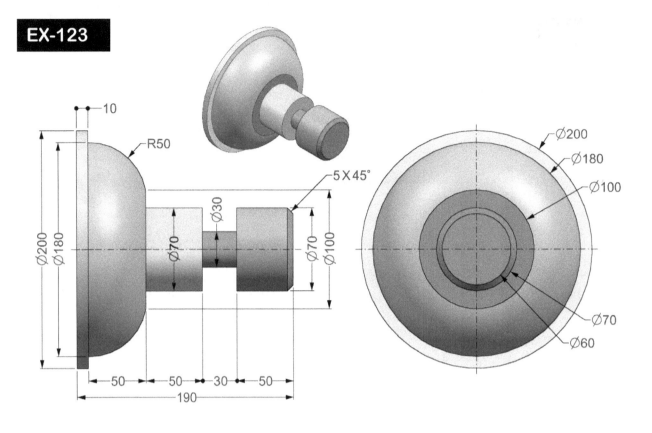

10
R50
5 × 45°
Ø30
Ø70
Ø70
Ø100
Ø200
Ø180
50
50
30
50
190

Ø200
Ø180
Ø100
Ø70
Ø60

EX-124

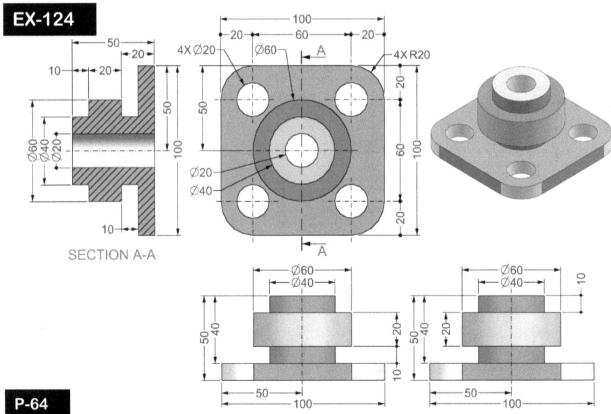

50
20
10
20
10
Ø60
Ø40
Ø20
50
100

SECTION A-A

100
20
60
20
4X Ø20
Ø60
A
4X R20
20
50
60
100
Ø20
Ø40
20
A

Ø60
Ø40
50
40
20
10
50
100

Ø60
Ø40
10
50
40
20
50
100

EX-125

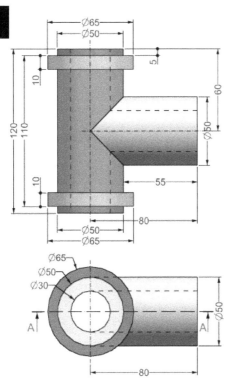

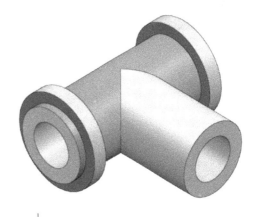

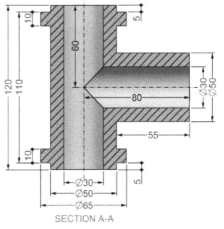

SECTION A-A

EX-126

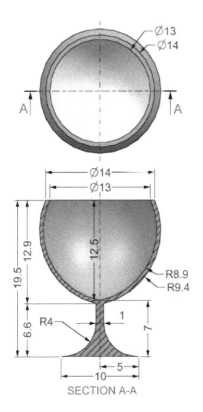

SECTION A-A

P-65

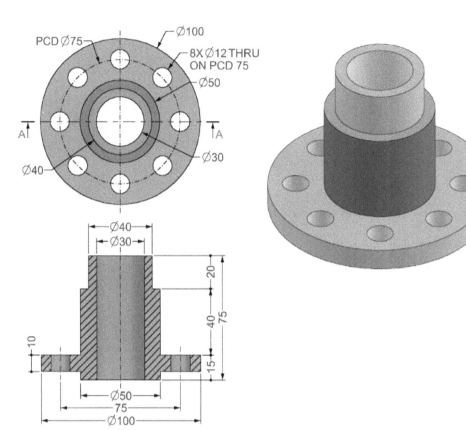

PCD Ø75
Ø100
8X Ø12 THRU
ON PCD 75
Ø50
Ø40
Ø30

A — A

Ø40
Ø30
20
40
75
10
15
Ø50
75
Ø100
SECTION A-A

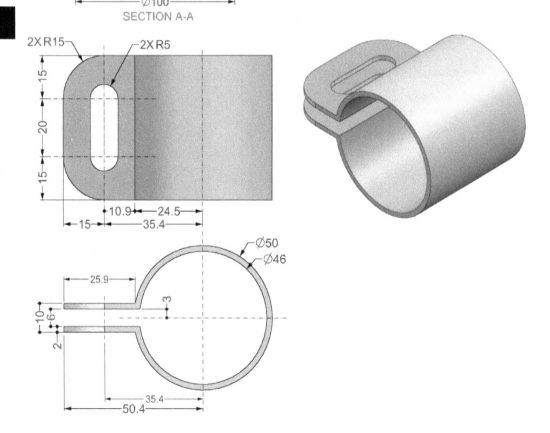

2X R15
2X R5
15
20
15
10.9
24.5
15
35.4

25.9
3
10
6
2
Ø50
Ø46
35.4
50.4

EX-129

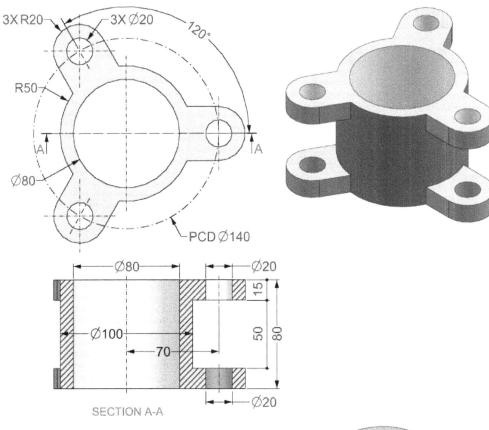

3X R20
3X Ø20
120°
R50
A
A
Ø80
PCD Ø140

Ø80
Ø20
15
Ø100
50
80
70
Ø20

SECTION A-A

EX-130

PCD Ø55
Ø70
A
A
8X Ø8
ON PCD 55
Ø30
Ø40

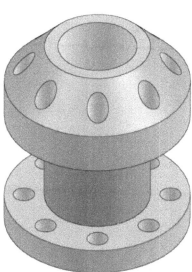

Ø40
45°
30
Ø8
Ø40
80
Ø8
35
15
10
Ø30
Ø40
PCD 55
Ø70

SECTION A-A

EX-131

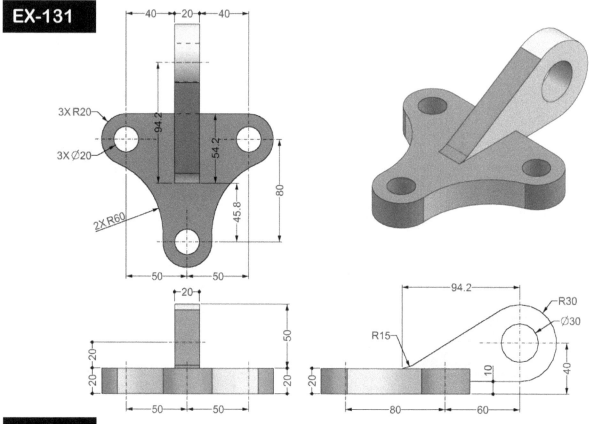

EX-132

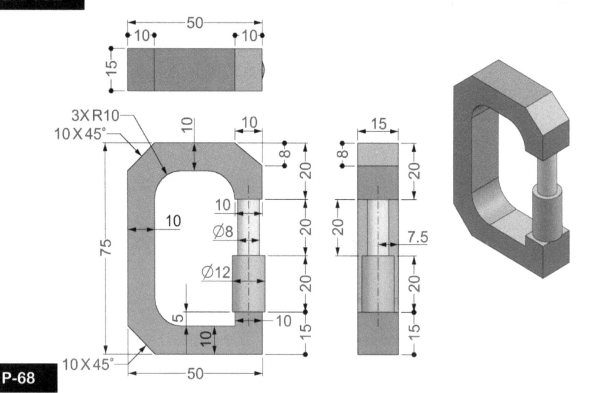

EX-133

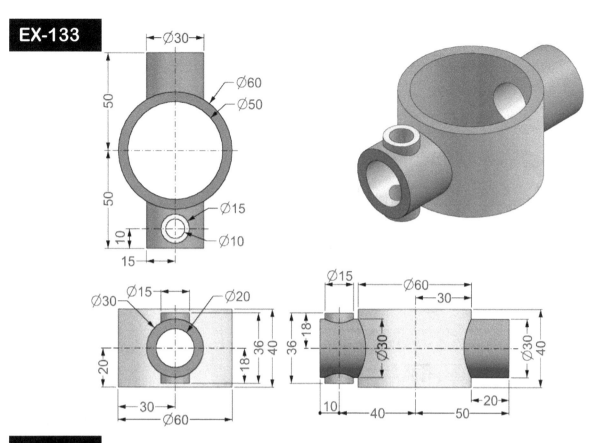

EX-134

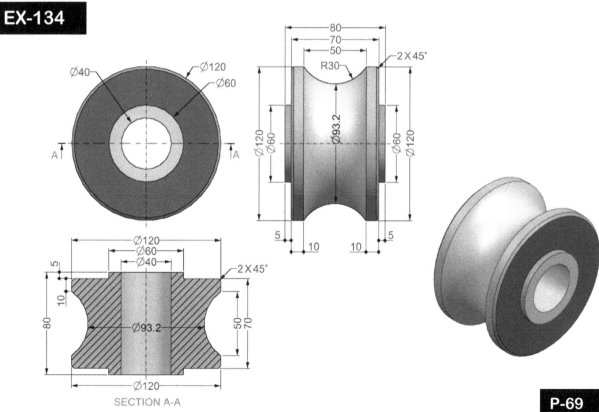

SECTION A-A

P-69

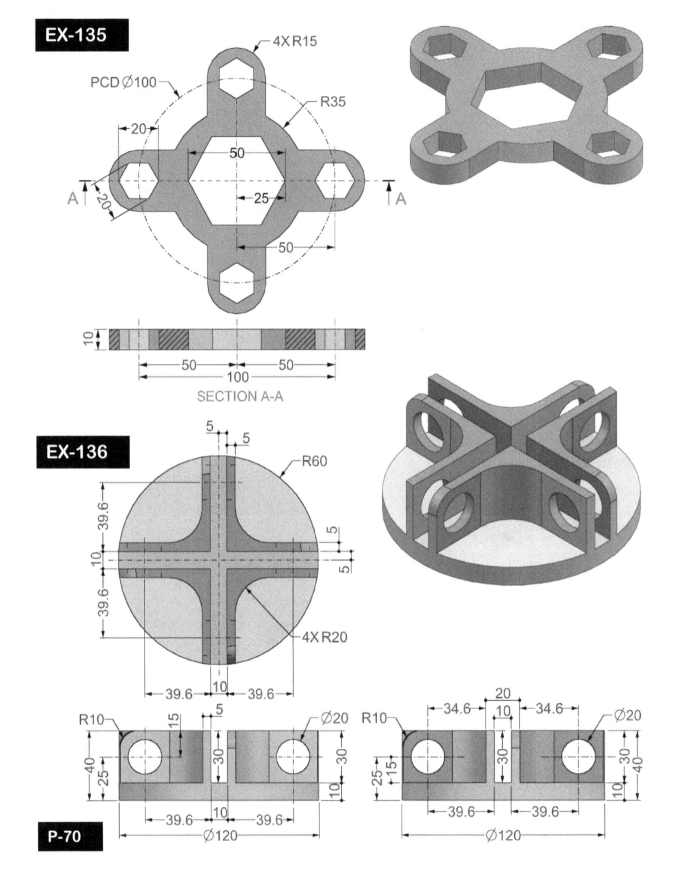

EX-135

4X R15

PCD Ø100

R35

20

50

25

50

A

20

A

50

10

50

50

100

SECTION A-A

EX-136

5

5

R60

39.6

10

5

39.6

5

4X R20

39.6

10

39.6

P-70

R10

15

5

Ø20

40

25

30

30

10

39.6

10

39.6

Ø120

R10

20

10

34.6

34.6

Ø20

25

15

30

30

40

10

39.6

39.6

Ø120

EX-137

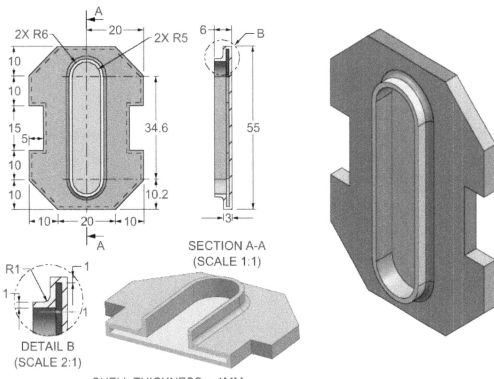

2X R6
2X R5
20
6
B

10
10
15
5
10
10
34.6
55
10.2

10
20
10
3

SECTION A-A
(SCALE 1:1)

R1
1
1
1

DETAIL B
(SCALE 2:1)

SHELL THICKNESS = 1MM
ALL INSIDE WALL THICKNESS

EX-138

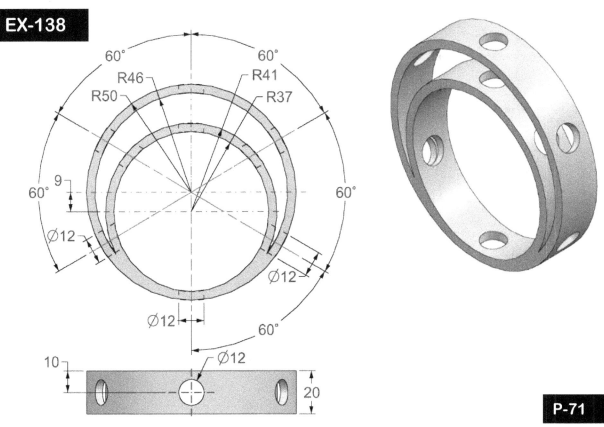

60°
60°
R46
R41
R50
R37

60°
9
60°

Ø12
Ø12
Ø12
60°

10
Ø12
20

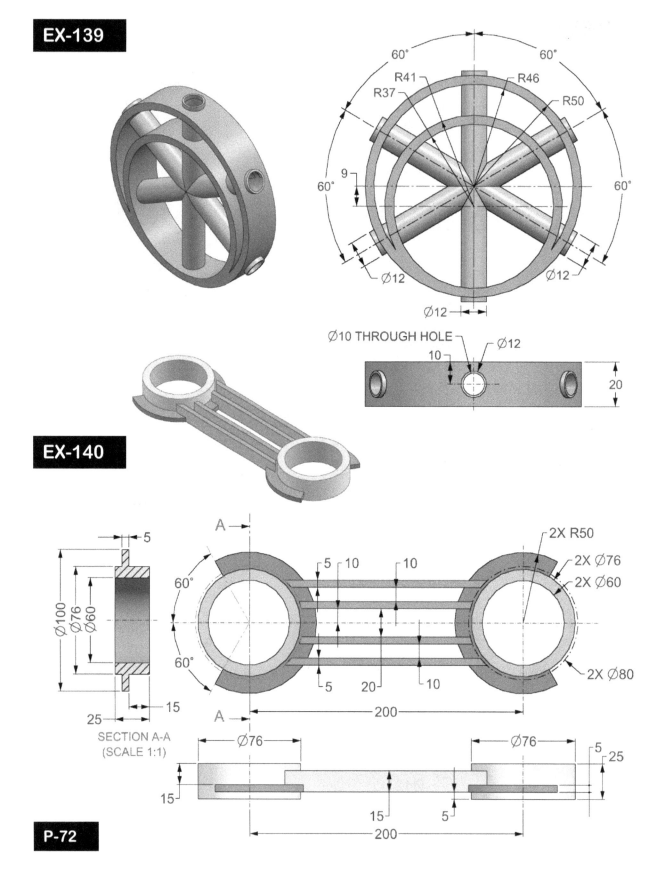

EX-139

R41
R37
R46
R50

60°
60°
60°
60°
60°
60°

9

Ø12
Ø12
Ø12

Ø10 THROUGH HOLE
Ø12
10
20

EX-140

SECTION A-A
(SCALE 1:1)

A
A

Ø100
Ø76
Ø60

5
15
25

60°
60°

5
10
10
5
20
10

2X R50
2X Ø76
2X Ø60
2X Ø80

200

Ø76
Ø76
5
25
15
15
5
200

P-72

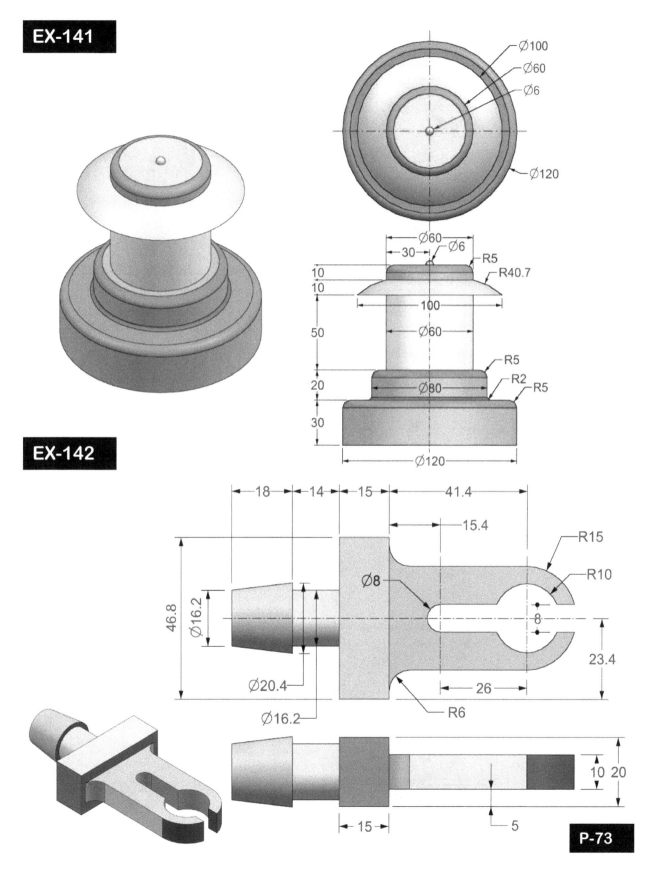

EX-141

⌀100
⌀60
⌀6
⌀120

⌀60
30
⌀6
R5
R40.7
10
10
100
50
⌀60
20
R5
R2 R5
⌀80
30
⌀120

EX-142

18
14
15
41.4
15.4
R15
R10
⌀8
8
46.8
⌀16.2
⌀20.4
23.4
⌀16.2
26
R6

10 20
15
5

P-73

EX-143

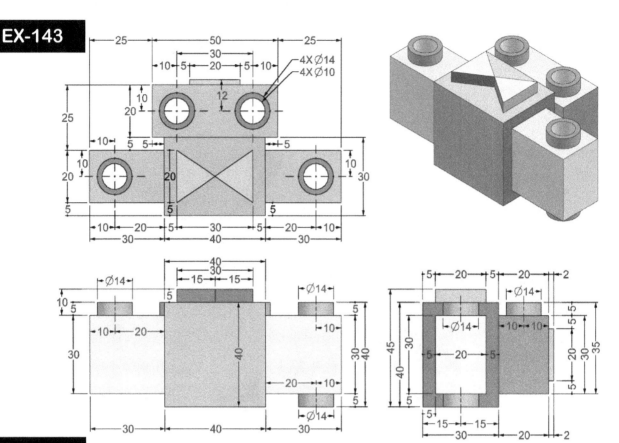

EX-144

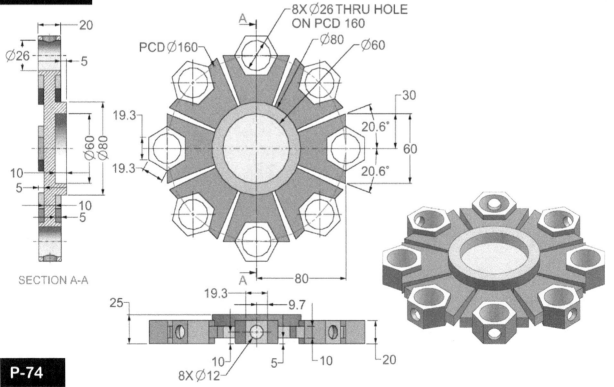

8X Ø26 THRU HOLE
ON PCD 160

PCD Ø160   Ø80   Ø60

SECTION A-A

8X Ø12

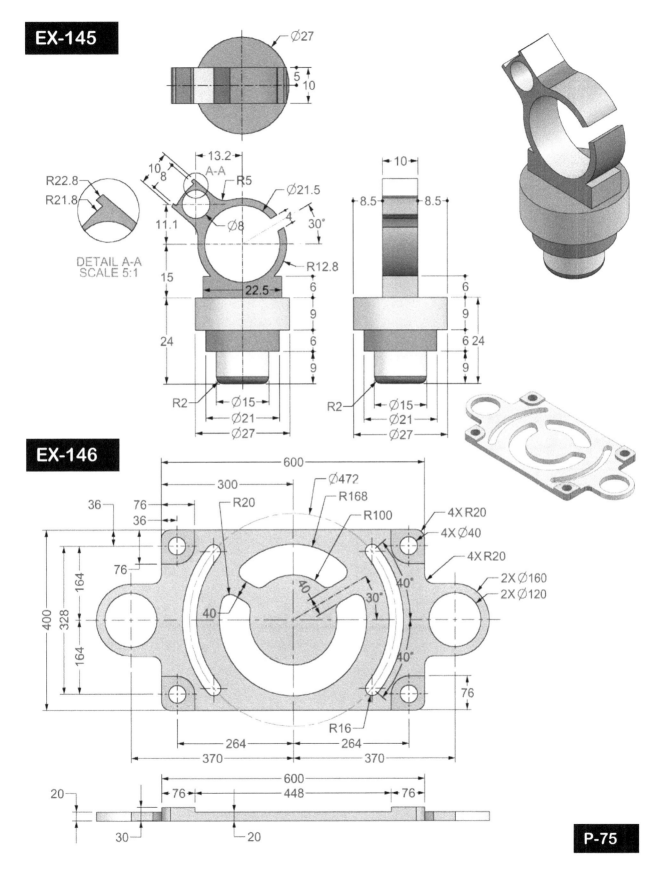

EX-145

Ø27
5
10

13.2
10
8
A-A
R5
Ø21.5
R22.8
R21.8
11.1
Ø8
4
30°
DETAIL A-A
SCALE 5:1
R12.8
15
22.5
6
9
24
6
9
R2
Ø15
Ø21
Ø27

10
8.5   8.5
6
9
6 24
9
R2
Ø15
Ø21
Ø27

EX-146

600
300
Ø472
R168
R20
R100
36
76
4X R20
36
4X Ø40
76
4X R20
164
40
40°
2X Ø160
400
328
40
30°
2X Ø120
164
40
40°
76
R16
264
264
370
370

600
76
448
76
20
30
20

P-75

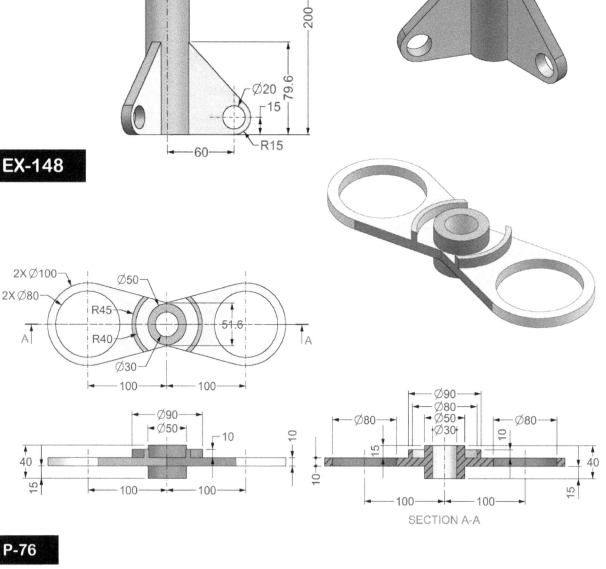

EX-147

∅40
120°
∅20
120°
10
60

R10
∅40
200
79.6
∅20
15
R15
60

EX-148

2X ∅100
2X ∅80
∅50
R45
R40
∅30
A
A
51.6
100
100

∅90
∅50
10
10
40
15
100
100

∅90
∅80
∅50
∅30
∅80
∅80
15
10
10
40
15
100
100
SECTION A-A

P-76

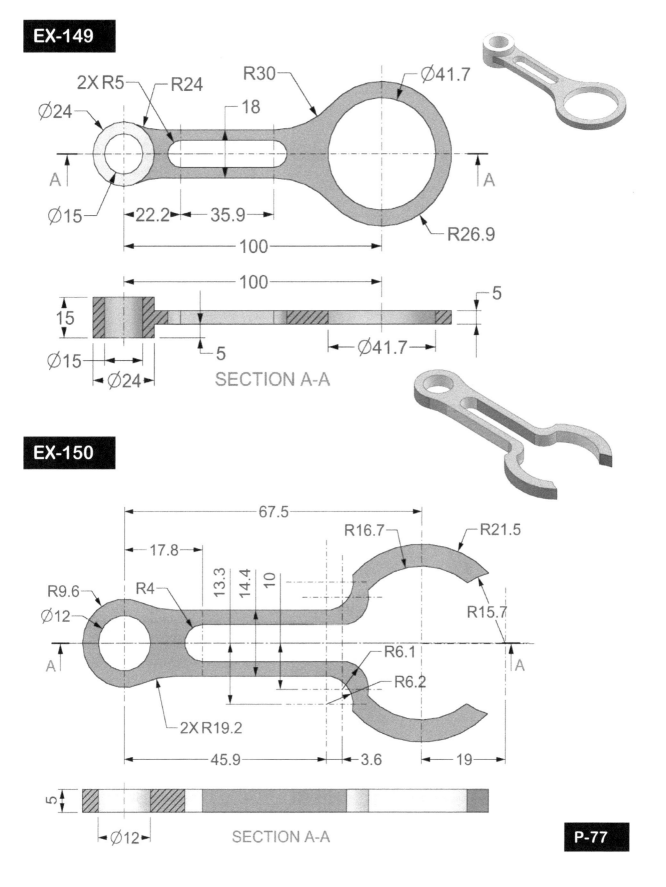

EX-149

2X R5 — R24 R30 — Ø41.7

Ø24

18

A

A

Ø15

2X R5

22.2 — 35.9

100

R26.9

100

15

5

Ø15

5

Ø41.7

Ø24

SECTION A-A

EX-150

67.5

17.8

R16.7 — R21.5

13.3 14.4 10

R9.6

R4

R15.7

Ø12

A

A

R6.1

R6.2

2X R19.2

45.9 3.6 19

5

Ø12

SECTION A-A

EX-151

Ø8
6,5
10
28
R1.5
R1.5
11
B-B
27
Ø10

SECTION A-A

Ø20
A
R3
35
15°
20
5
A
Ø13.3
Ø16

R8
R6.7
R10
R4
R5

DETAIL B-B
SCALE 5:1
45°
1

EX-152

Ø20
Ø36
Ø58
Ø52
Ø16

Ø36
Ø20
R8
8
2
135°
Ø16
R11.2
76
21,6
13
20
13.5
15.8
10.7
10
R6
Ø16
R3

SECTION A-A

A
58
3
R3
R2
Ø52
76
R6
A
40

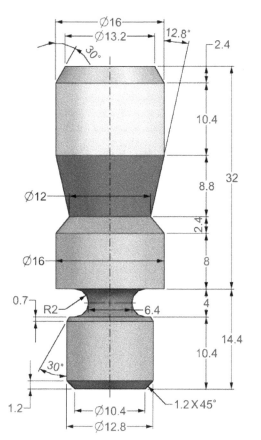

Ø16
Ø13.2
12.8°
2.4
30°
10.4
8.8
32
Ø12
2.4
Ø16
8
4
0.7
R2
6.4
14.4
10.4
30°
1.2
Ø10.4
1.2 X 45°
Ø12.8

EX-154

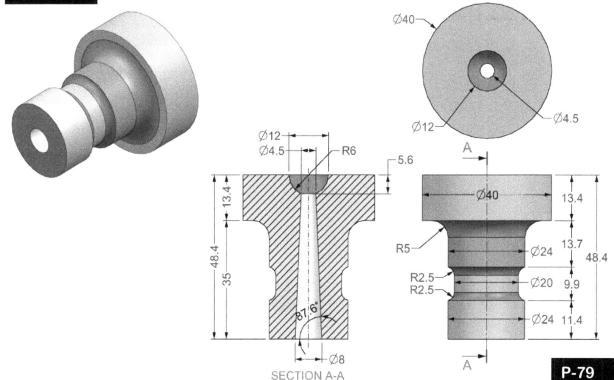

Ø40
Ø12
Ø4.5

Ø12
Ø4.5
R6
5.6
13.4
48.4
35
87.6°
Ø8
SECTION A-A

A

Ø40
13.4
R5
13.7
Ø24
R2.5
Ø20
9.9
R2.5
48.4
Ø24
11.4

A

P-79

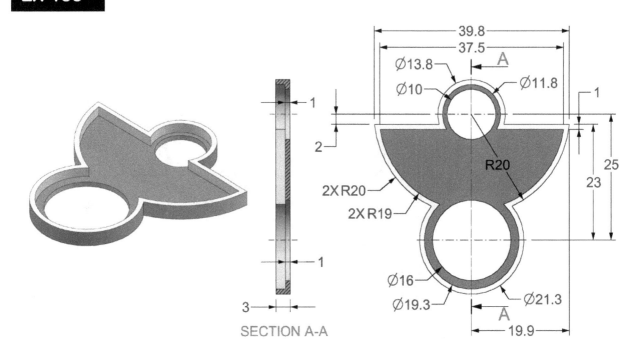

SECTION A-A

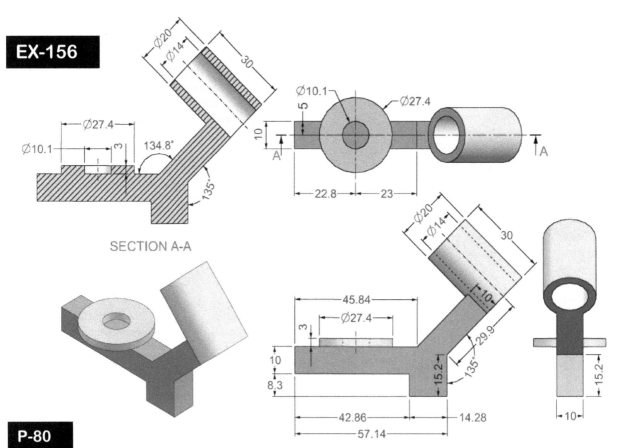

SECTION A-A

EX-157

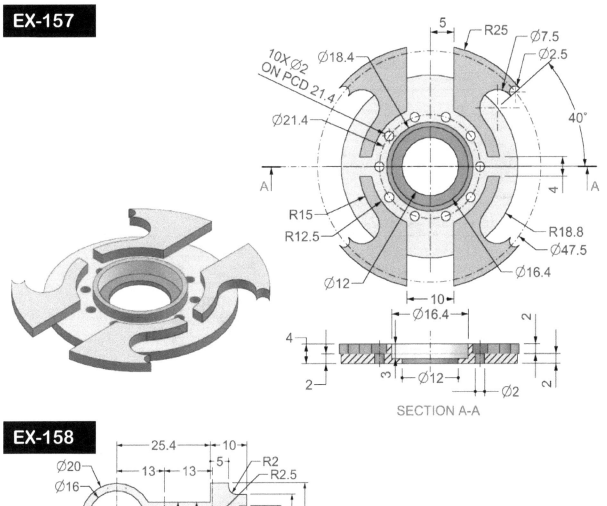

SECTION A-A

EX-158

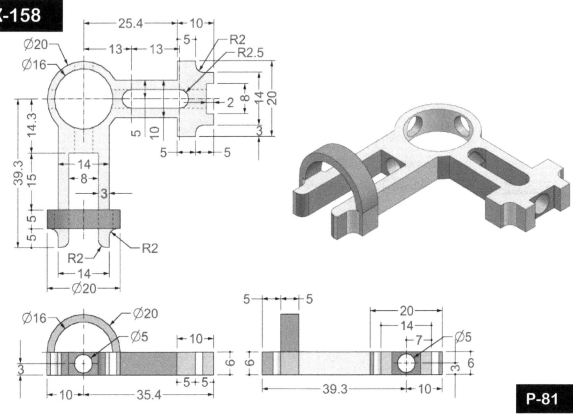

P-81

EX-159

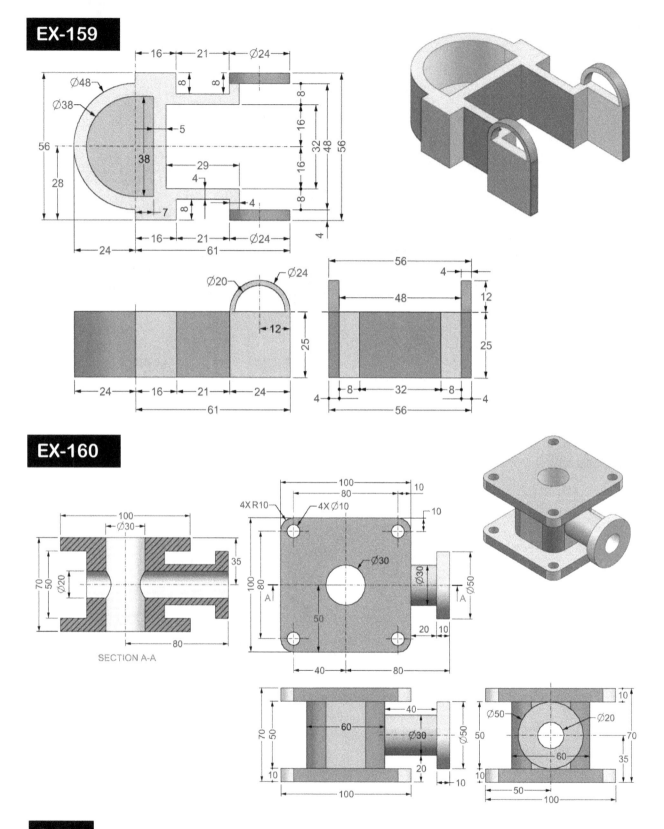

EX-160

SECTION A-A

4X R10 4X Ø10

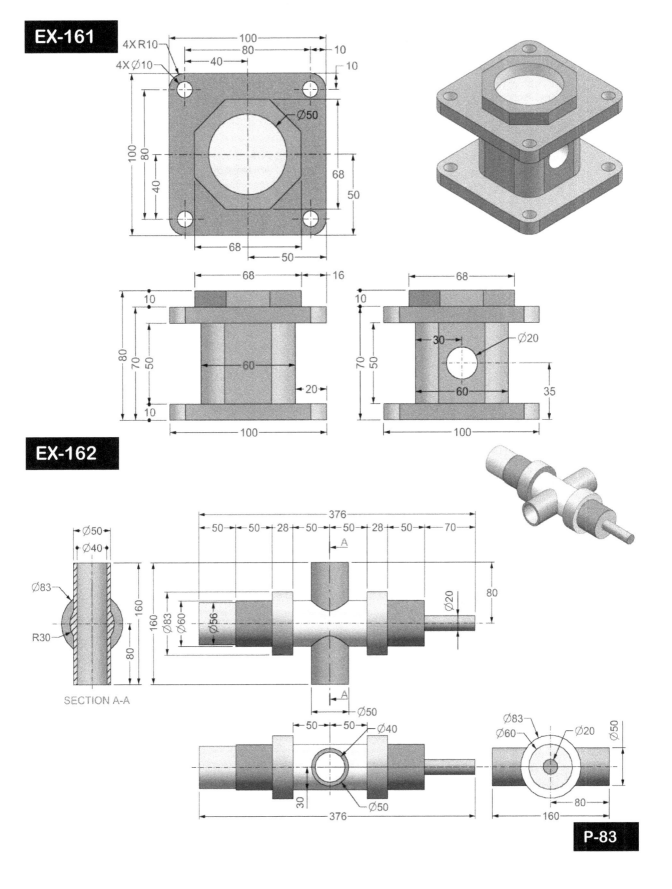

EX-161

4X R10
4X Ø10
100
80
40
10
10
Ø50
100
80
40
68
50
68
50

68
16
10
80
70
50
60
20
10
100

68
10
70
50
30
Ø20
60
35
100

EX-162

376
50
50
28
50
50
28
50
70
A
Ø50
Ø40
80
Ø83
160
160
Ø83
Ø60
Ø56
Ø20
R30
80
A
SECTION A-A

Ø50
50
50
Ø40
Ø83
Ø60
Ø20
Ø50
30
160
80
Ø50
376

P-83

EX-163

PCD Ø160
4X Ø20
2X Ø20
2X R10
R100
Ø40
Ø20
2X Ø14 THRU HOLES
PCD Ø80.5
Ø120

TOP VIEW

Ø20
Ø20
Ø20
10
20

SECTION A-A

10
20
Ø10

SECTION B-B

Ø20
Ø40

BOTTOM VIEW

10
Ø20
Ø20
Ø20
20

SECTION C-C

EX-164

68
28.2
4X R10
4X Ø10
10
Ø50
Ø30
68
28.2
80
100
40
10
10
40
40
10
80
100

16
68
28.2
16
10 10
80
70
50
Ø18
25
30
10
60
35
50
100

100
68
Ø50
10
10 10
Ø18
50
25
Ø30
10
50
50
100

SECTION A-A

P-84

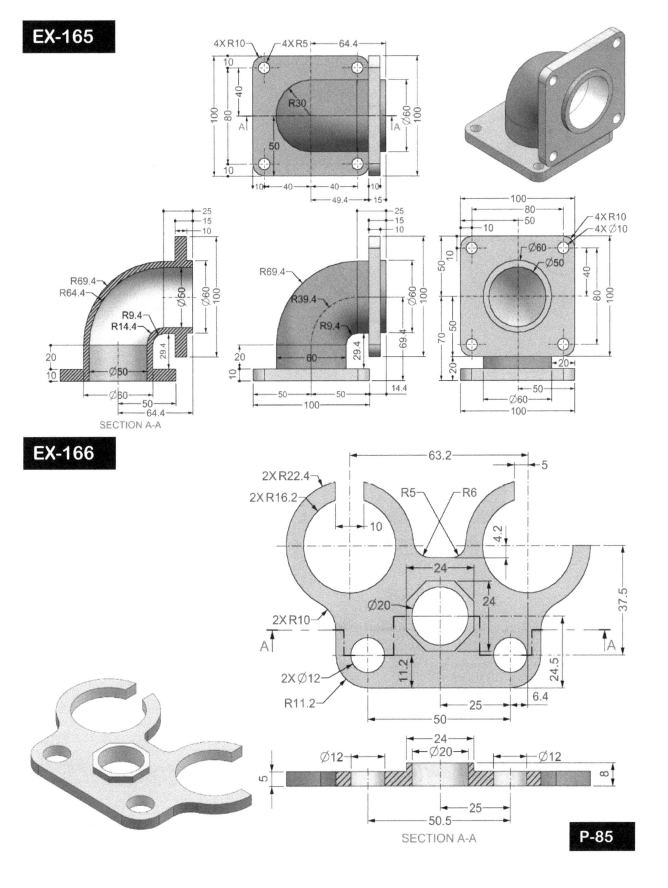

EX-165

4X R10   4X R5   64.4
10
40
80
100   R30
A |A   Ø60   100
50
10
10   40   40   10
49.4   15

25
15
10
R69.4
R64.4   Ø50   Ø60   100
R9.4
R14.4   29.4
20
10   Ø50
Ø60
50
64.4
SECTION A-A

25
15
10
R69.4
R39.4   Ø60   100
R9.4   69.4
29.4
20
10   60
50   50   14.4
100

100
80
50
10   4X R10
4X Ø10
Ø60
50   Ø50
10
50   40
80
70   100
20
20
50
Ø60
100

EX-166

63.2   5
2X R22.4
2X R16.2   R5   R6
10   4.2
24
Ø20   24
2X R10
A |A
11.2   24.5
2X Ø12
R11.2   6.4
25   37.5
50

24
Ø12   Ø20   Ø12
5   8
25
50.5
SECTION A-A

P-85

EX-167

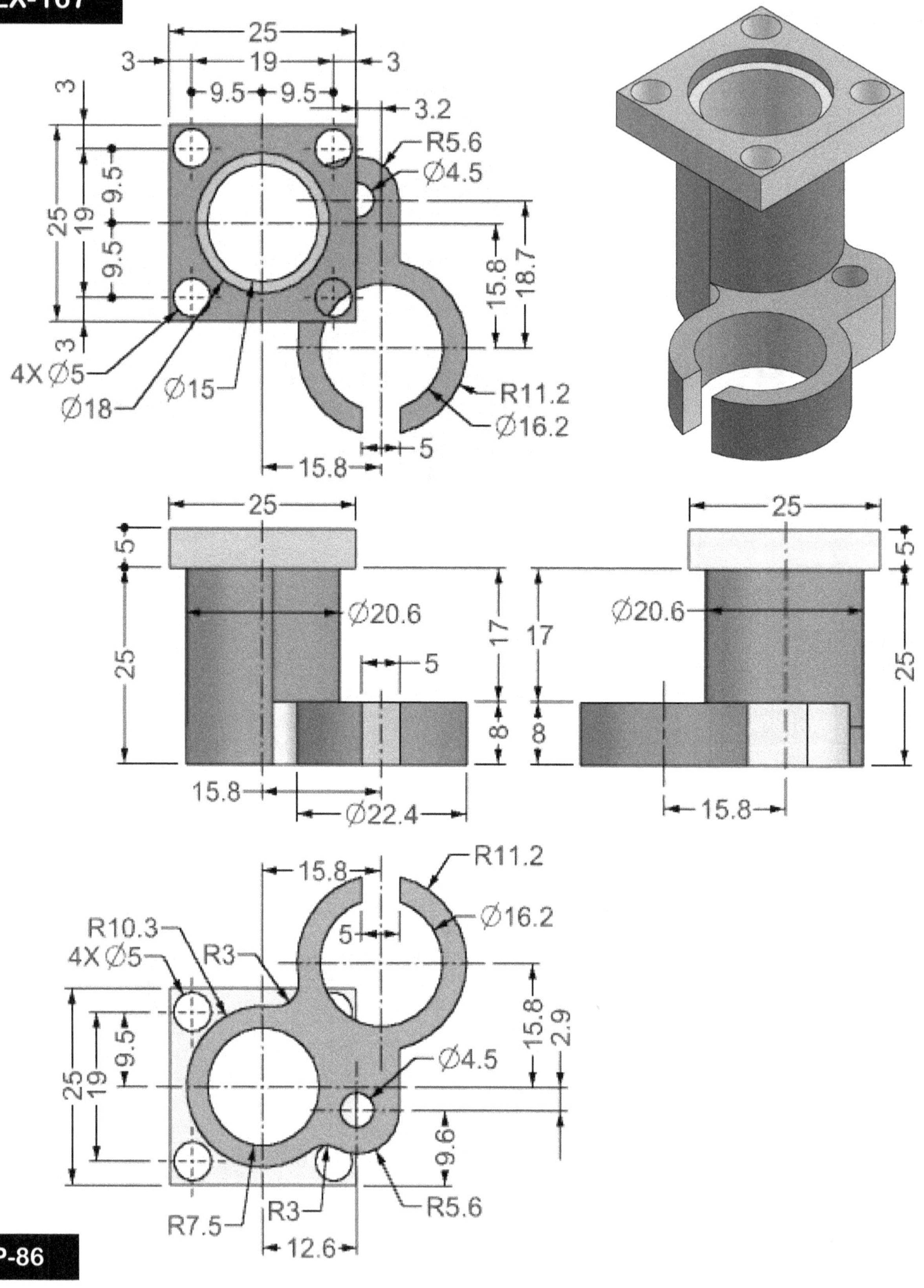

25
3
19
3
9.5
9.5
3.2
R5.6
⌀4.5
25
19
9.5
9.5
3
3
15.8
18.7
4X ⌀5
⌀18
⌀15
R11.2
⌀16.2
5
15.8
25
5
⌀20.6
17
25
5
8
15.8
⌀22.4
25
5
⌀20.6
17
25
8
15.8
R11.2
15.8
⌀16.2
R10.3
4X ⌀5
5
R3
15.8
2.9
25
19
9.5
⌀4.5
9.6
R7.5
R3
R5.6
12.6

EX-168

PCD Ø95
Ø120
8X Ø14
8X Ø10
ON PCD 95
R35
R25
6
3
A — A

32
30
80 16
20
2
32
Ø70
Ø120

30
Ø14
Ø10
16 20
Ø50
Ø70
PCD 95
Ø120

SECTION A-A

EX-169

Ø70
Ø40
20
40
R5
Ø28
Ø40
50
130
70
200

Ø70
R2
R60
Ø80
R5
30
21.3
40
50
80
140
30
Ø28
Ø40
10
50
80
70

Ø70
15 40 15
10
30
Ø28
Ø40
80
15
15
70
30
35
Ø70

P-87

EX-170

4X R2
3
2X Ø3
2.75 — 4.75 — Ø15 — 4.75 — 2.75
1 — 1
4
6
30

R7.5 — R6.5
8.5
R2
R2
13
8.5 — 8.5
15
30

1 — 1
7.5
16
4
8.5
1
1
6

EX-171

44 — 184 — 44
22 — 92 — 22
4X Ø23.2
R60
138.6
30
30
30
30
30
20
138.6
248
168
40
40
124
40
80
228
272

44 — 20 — 40 — 44
40
20
35
40
264
272

P-88

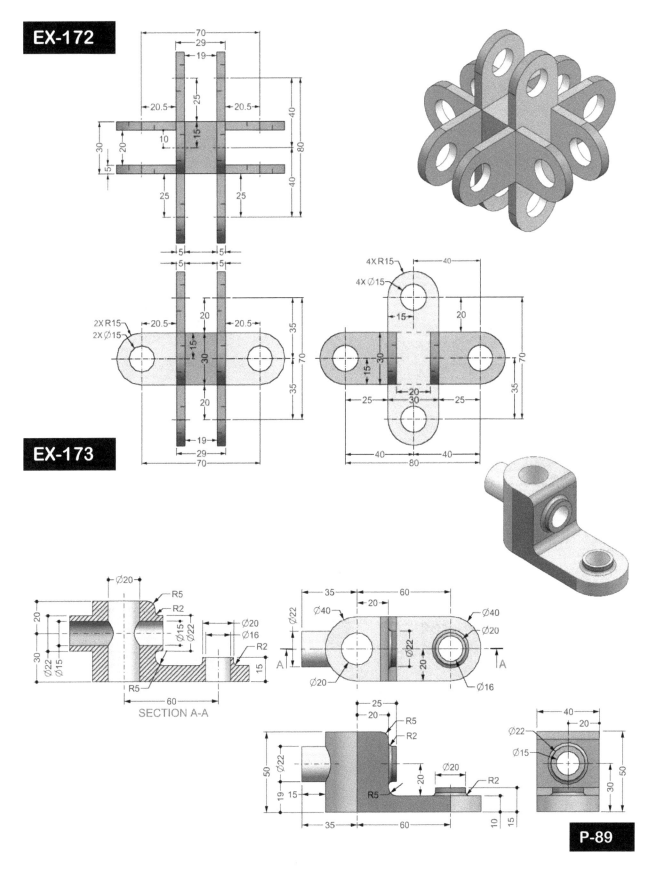

EX-172

EX-173

SECTION A-A

P-89

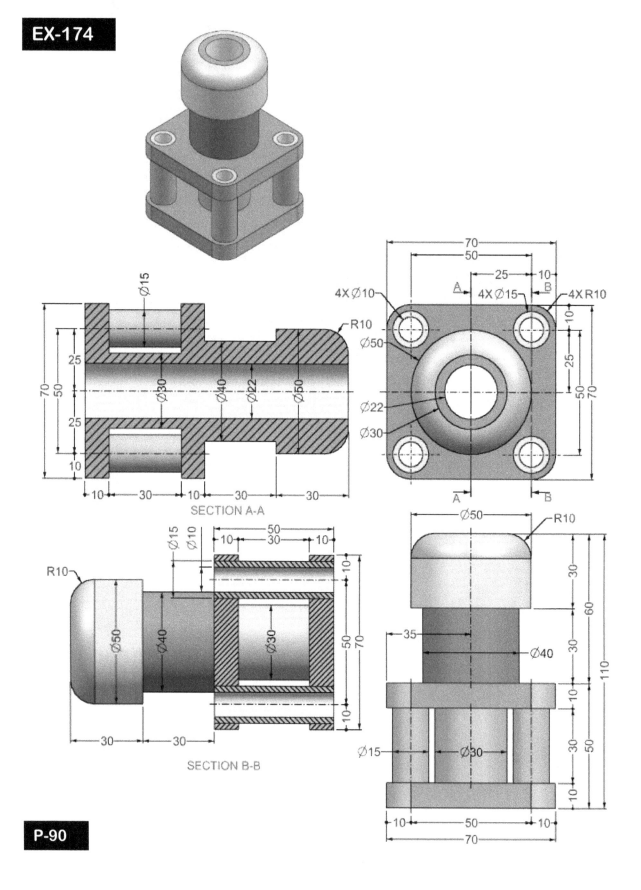

EX-174

P-90

Ø15

70
50
25
25
10

Ø30
Ø40
Ø22
Ø50

R10

10 — 30 — 10 — 30 — 30

SECTION A-A

70
50
25
10
4X Ø10
R10
Ø50
Ø22
Ø30
A
4X Ø15
B
4X R10
10
25
50
70
A
B

Ø15
Ø10
50
10 — 30 — 10
R10
Ø50
Ø40
Ø30
10
50
70
10
30 — 30

SECTION B-B

Ø50
R10
30
60
35
Ø40
30
10
110
Ø15
Ø30
30
50
10
10 — 50 — 10
70

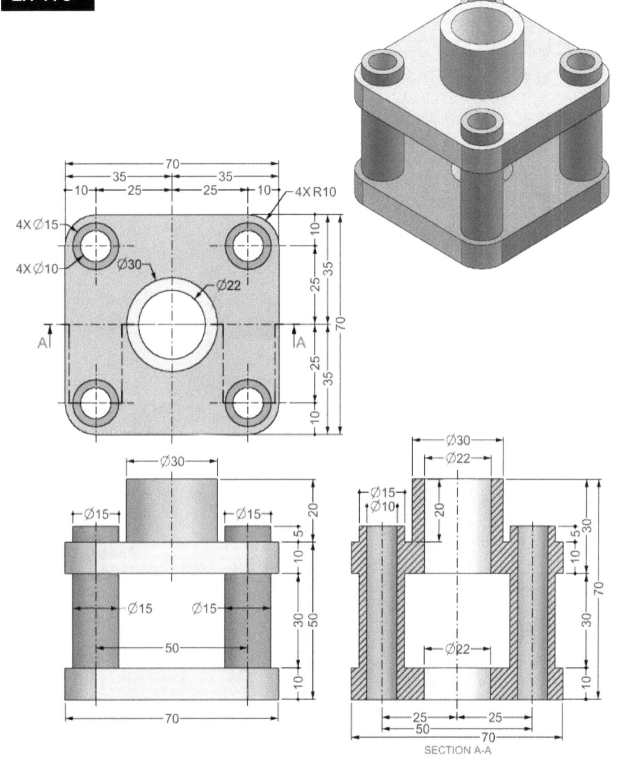

4X Ø15
4X Ø10
4X R10
Ø30
Ø22

70
35
35
10
25
25
10
10
25
35
70
25
35
10

A
A

Ø30
Ø15
Ø15
20
5
10
30
50
10
Ø15
Ø15
50
70

Ø30
Ø22
Ø15
Ø10
20
5
10
30
70
30
10
Ø22
25
25
50
70

SECTION A-A

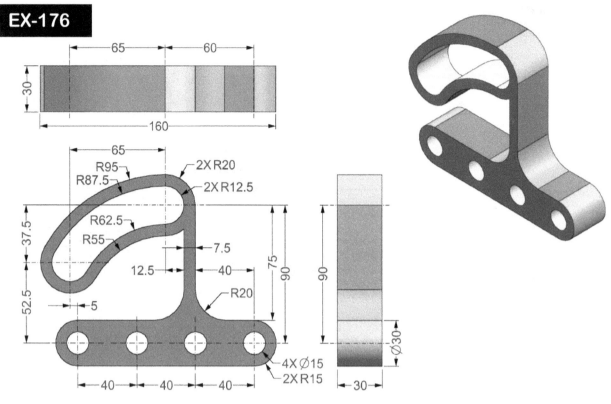

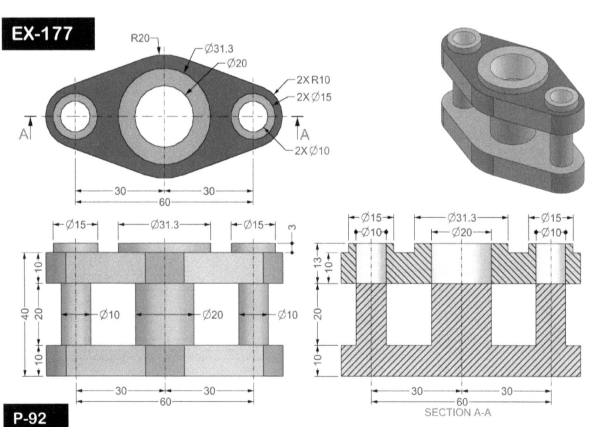

SECTION A-A

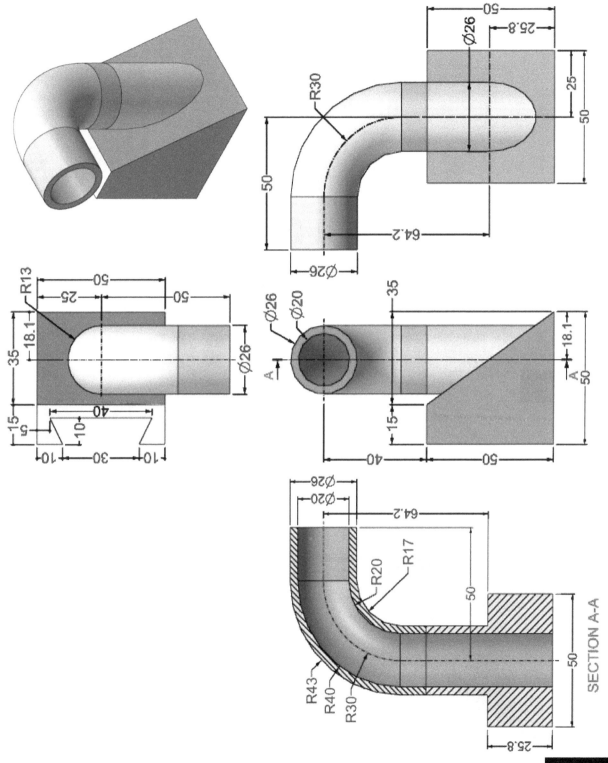

EX-178

R30

Ø26

50

25.8

25

50

64.2

Ø26

R13

R30

Ø26

Ø20

50

25

50

Ø26

35

18.1

35

A

18.1

50

15

15

5

40

10

10

30

40

50

Ø26

Ø20

64.2

R20

R17

50

R43

R40

R30

50

25.8

SECTION A-A

P-93

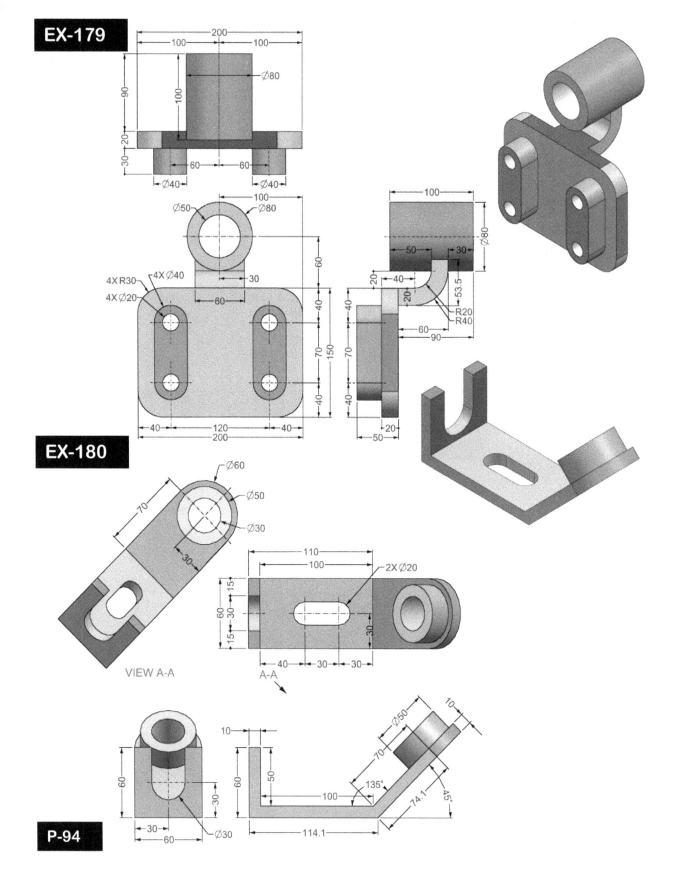

EX-179

EX-180

VIEW A-A

A-A

P-94

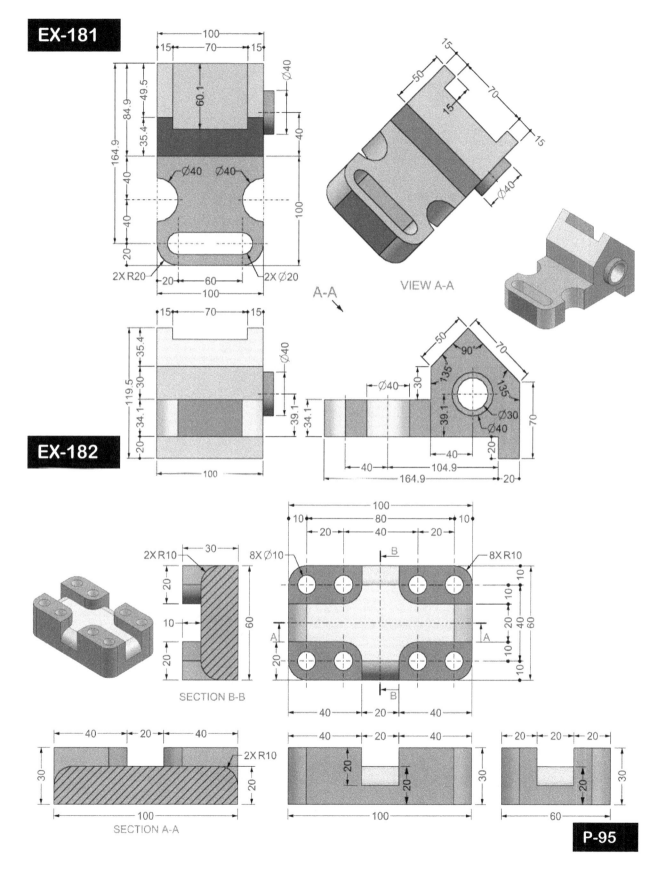

EX-181

EX-182

A-A

VIEW A-A

SECTION B-B

SECTION A-A

P-95

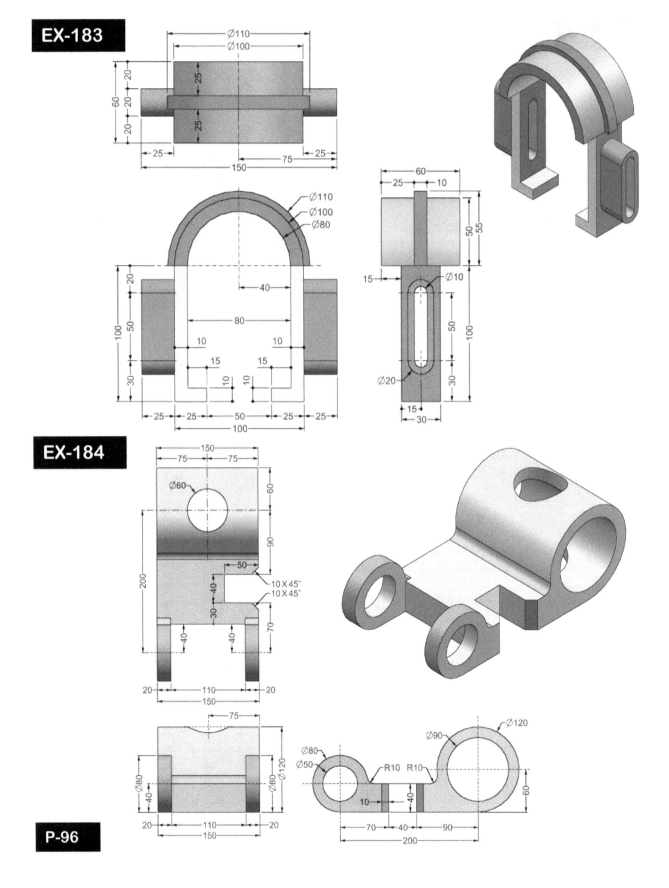

EX-183

EX-184

P-96

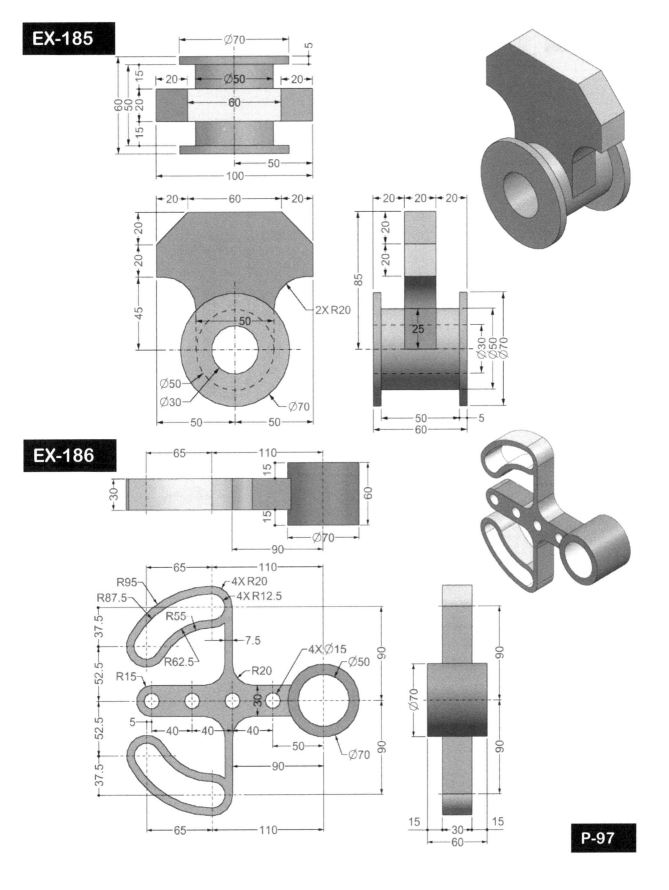

EX-185

EX-186

P-97

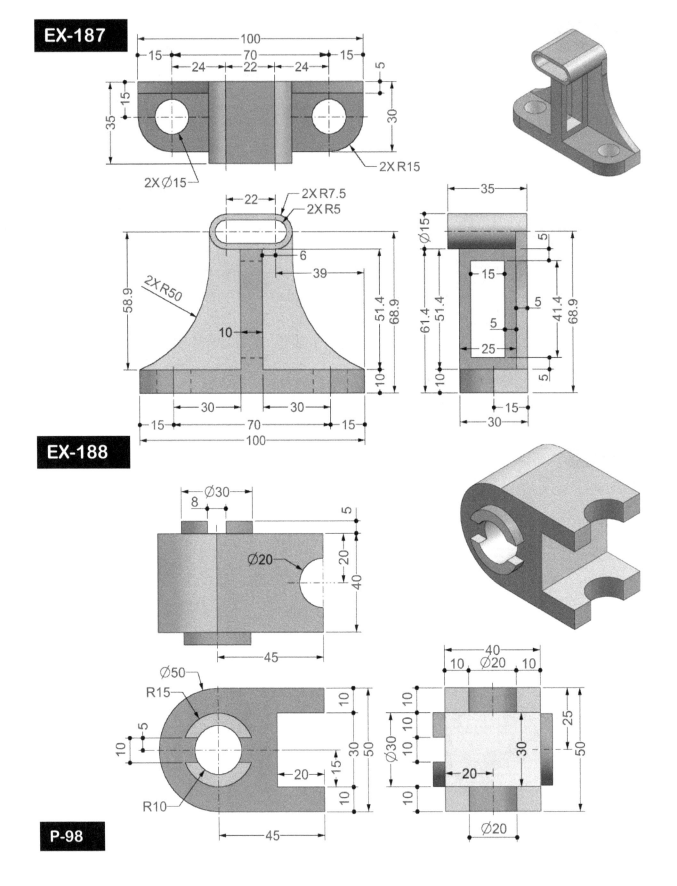

EX-187

EX-188

P-98

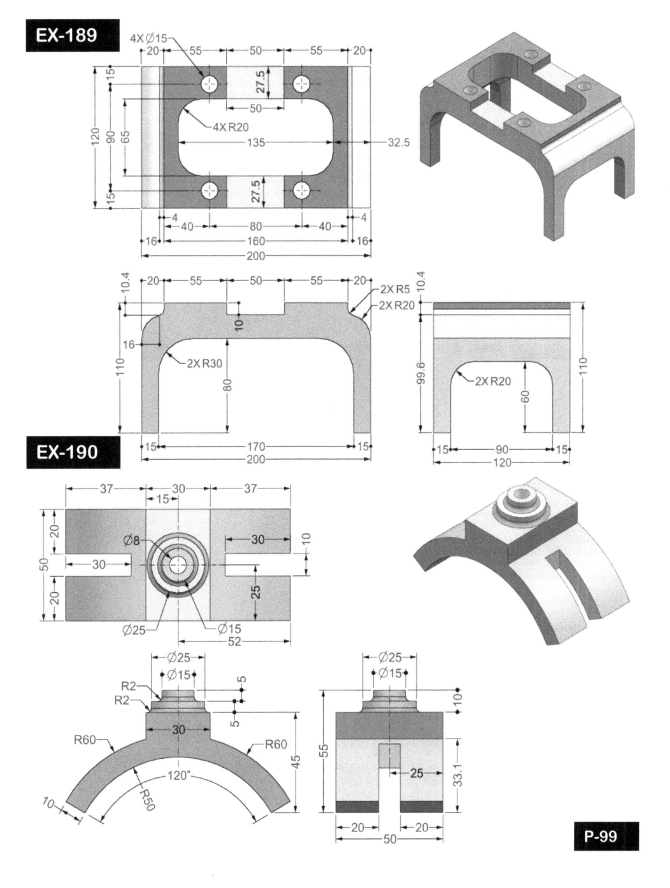

EX-189

4X Ø15
20 55 50 55 20
15
27.5
120 90 65
50
4X R20
135 32.5
15
27.5
4
40 80 40
4
16 160 16
200

20 55 50 55 20
10.4 10.4
2X R5
2X R20
16
110
10
2X R30
80
99.6 110
2X R20
60
15 170 15
15 90 15
200
120

EX-190

37 30 37
15
20
Ø8
50 30 30 10
20 25
Ø25 Ø15
52

Ø25
Ø15
R2
5
R2
5
R60 30 R60
45
120°
R50
10

Ø25
Ø15
10
55
33.1
25
20 20
50

P-99

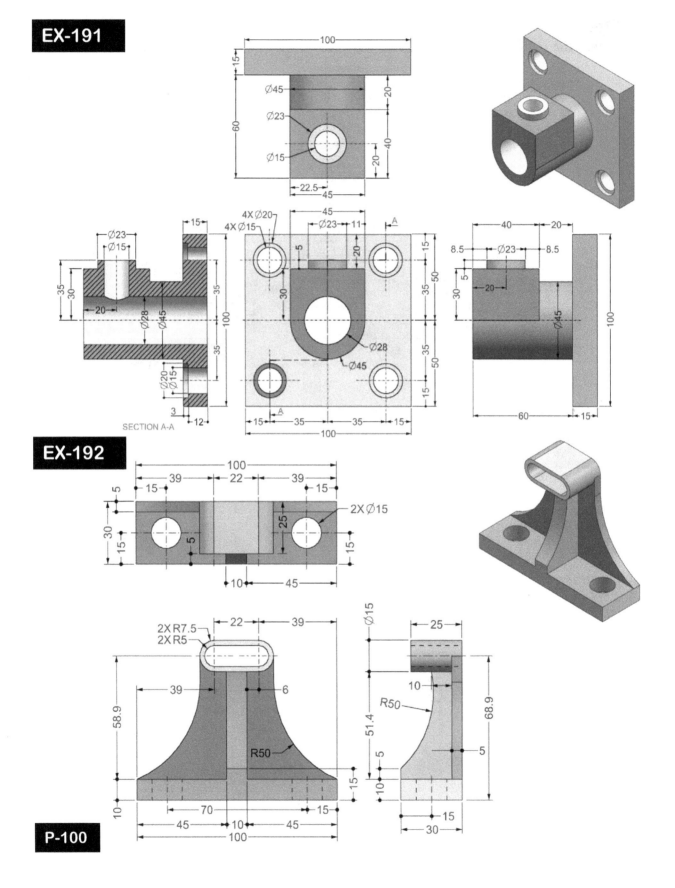

EX-191

EX-192

P-100

EX-193

SECTION A-A

- 40
- 12
- 10
- 10
- 80
- 60
- 10
- R2
- Ø20
- Ø30
- 1 x 45°
- 30
- Ø8
- Ø14

- Ø30
- 15
- 40
- 2X Ø14
- 2X R10
- 2X Ø8
- R20
- 30
- 60
- 30
- 10
- Ø20
- Ø30
- 55
- A — A

- Ø30
- Ø23
- R2
- R2
- Ø30
- Ø14
- 40
- 15
- 10
- 12
- 55

- 40
- Ø30
- Ø14
- 20
- R3.2
- 40
- 10
- 12
- 30
- 30
- 60

EX-194

- 150
- 4X Ø20
- 20
- 110
- 20
- 55
- 20
- 40
- R5
- 40
- 15
- 15
- 130
- 30
- 60
- Ø120
- 40
- 30
- 35
- 40
- 70
- 40

ALL HOLES CHAMFER 2MM

- 130°
- 2X Ø20
- 2X Ø50
- 25°
- Ø120
- Ø100
- R5
- 75
- PCD Ø160
- R5
- 40
- R5
- 80
- 40
- 70
- 40
- 35
- 20

- 60
- 30
- 15
- 80
- 30
- 40
- R5
- 20
- 40
- 130

- 70
- 50
- 60
- 4X Ø20
- 20
- 20
- 110
- 150

BOTTOM VIEW

P-101

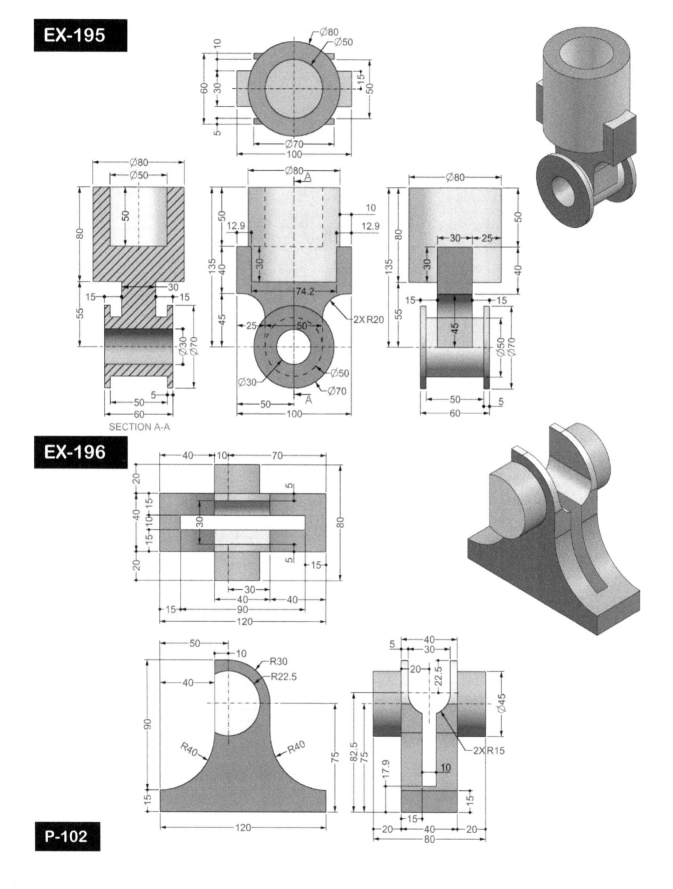

EX-195

Ø80
Ø50
10
60
30
15
50
5
Ø70
100

Ø80
Ø50
80
50
30
15
15
Ø30
Ø70
5
50
60
SECTION A-A

Ø80
A
10
50
12.9
12.9
135
30
40
74.2
45
2X R20
25
50
Ø30
Ø50
Ø70
50
A
100

Ø80
50
80
30 25
135
30
40
15 15
45
Ø50
Ø70
55
50
5
60

EX-196

40
10
70
20
5
40
15
10 15
30
80
15
15
20
5
30
15
40
40
15
90
120

50
10
R30
R22.5
40
90
R40
R40
75
15
120

5
40
30
20
22.5
Ø45
82.5
75
2X R15
17.9
10
15
15
20 40 20
80

P-102

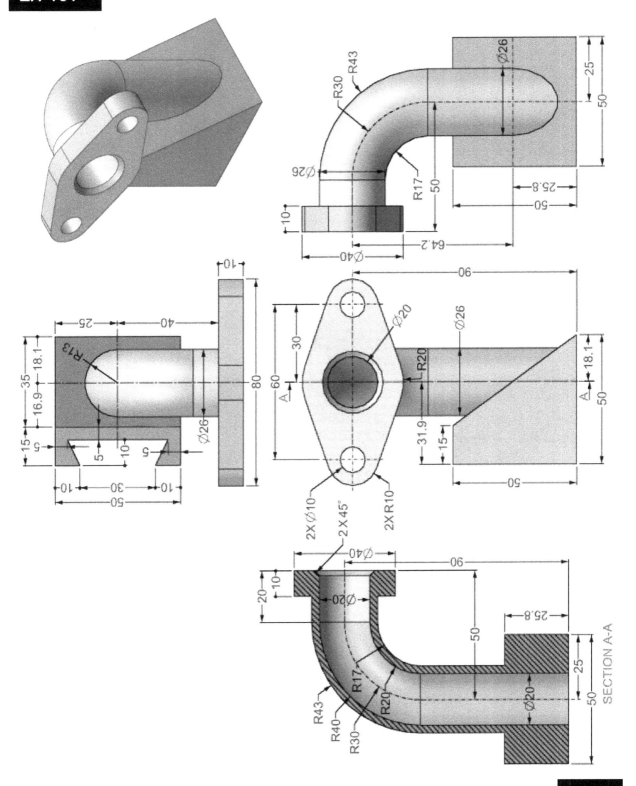

EX-197

P-103

6X Ø15 THRU
ON PCD 90
Ø120
Ø50
Ø40
PCD Ø90
A
A

Ø120
Ø50
Ø40
15
10
Ø15
120
30
60°
60°
80
Ø10
Ø20
Ø30
PCD 54
5
10

SECTION A-A

B-B

VIEW B-B

8X Ø10 THRU
ON PCD 54
Ø30
Ø70
Ø20
PCD 54

EX-199

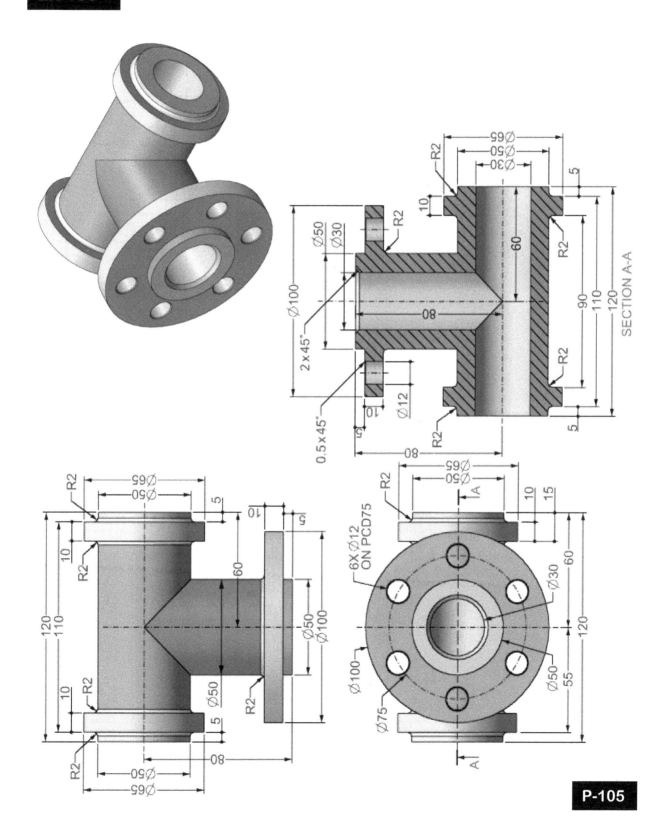

SECTION A-A

6X Ø12
ON PCD75

P-105

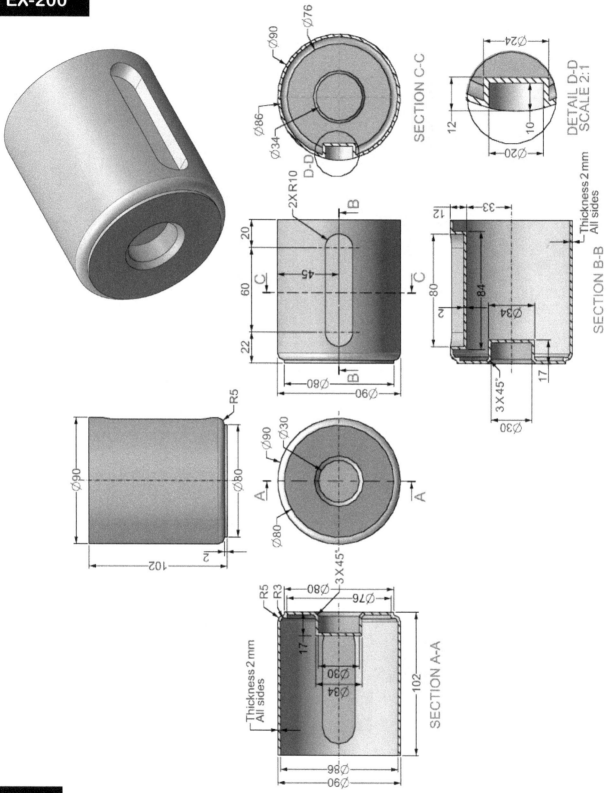

SECTION C-C

DETAIL D-D
SCALE 2:1

Ø24
Ø20
12
10

Ø90
Ø76
Ø86
Ø34
D-D

2XR10
20
60
22
45
Ø80
Ø90
B
C
C
B

SECTION B-B

12
33
80
84
Ø34
2
3 X 45°
17
Ø30
Thickness 2 mm
All sides

R5
Ø90
Ø80
102
2
A
A

Ø90
Ø30
Ø80

SECTION A-A

R5
R3
3 X 45°
Ø80
Ø76
17
Ø30
Ø84
102
Ø98
Ø90
Thickness 2 mm
All sides

Other useful books by CADIN360

1. 150 CAD Exercises

2. AutoCAD Exercises

3. CAD Exercises

4. 50+ SolidWorks Exercises

5. SolidWorks 200 Exercises

6. Autodesk Inventor Exercises

7. Catia Exercises

8. Siemens NX Exercises

www.ingramcontent.com/pod-product-compliance
Lightning Source LLC
Chambersburg PA
CBHW060448060326
40689CB00020B/4466